Focus On English©
Reference Series
Making the difficult parts of learning English easy!

Mastering English Prepositions for ESL Learners
Using Them Correctly in Every English Sentence

© Copyright 2008 by Thomas A. Celentano

All rights reserved.

No part of this book may be reproduced or transmitted in any form without the express written permission of the copyright holder.

All inquiries should be addressed to:

Focus On English
P.O. Box 1554
Kailua, Hawaii 96734
http://www.FOEBooks.com

ISBN **978-0-557-01752-2**

To my ESL students everywhere.

Mastering English Prepositions for ESL Learners
Using Them Correctly in Every English Sentence

This easy to use reference text about prepositions is designed for ESL Learners who want to clearly understand the use of prepositions in a wide variety of English sentences.

Why do we say: a person gets **on** a bus and **into** a taxi, **on** a plane and **into** a car; we arrive **in** New York **at** Kennedy Airport **on** Wednesday **at** 3pm **in** November; we sit **at** a desk but we sit **in** a chair; our hands are **on** the desk but our pencil is **in** our hand; we say we did something **for** him and then did something **to** him; I like my friend because he's **like** my brother; we have been talking **about** school **since** 2pm **for** 3 hours **outside** the building that is **close to** the bank; the book is **underneath** the counter, **beneath** the bookshelf, **under** the window, **near** the door, **beside** the TV, which is **next to** the chair that is **over** the box that is **on** the floor . . . whew!

Does some of this sound confusing to you? Well, don't worry! This Focus On English lesson is about English prepositions and will help you to understand and use English prepositions correctly in every situation.

If you would like to listen to this lesson on your iPod®, mp3 player, or computer, then you will be happy to know that this entire book is available as an audio book for your iPod or other mp3 player (available separately from your school store or from www.FOEBooks.com).

How to use this book

This book was designed to be a reference book that can be quickly searched for resources that will aid the student in understanding the correct use of prepositions in most English sentences. The reader will notice large page numbers at the top of each page which correspond to the detailed table of contents section beginning on page vii. At the back of the book there is an index where the student can quickly find prepositions that are of interest. The large format page numbers at the top of the book were designed to facilitate quick searches from the table of contents and the index.

Mastering Prepositions is broken down into three sections.

The **first section** provides the student with the resources to understand the functional use of prepositions in real English communication. In this section, the student will find explanations and examples relating to preposition usage in real situations.

The **second section** is designed to be a resource to help the student with the difficult area of prepositions following certain common verbs in English. The student may search this second section quickly by verb or by preposition to learn the correct verb/preposition combinations.

The **third section** is designed to be a reference resource for all of the most common prepositions used in English. This section contains a comprehensive listing of the prepositions followed by explanations and examples.

This book was designed so that the student could use it as a contiguous study text or as a resource manual.

A note to students

This book is available in its entirety as an mp3 audio book for iPods® and other mp3 players. To obtain a copy, please go to your school store or to www.FOEBooks.com.

Table of Contents

Section 1 ... 1

Understanding how to use English prepositions in everyday English

- **Chapter 1:** Using prepositions to talk about time. . . 2

    - Using *on* when talking about time. . . 2
    - Using *at* when talking about time. . . 2
    - Using *in* when talking about time. . . 3
    - Using *within* when talking about time. . . 5
    - Using *under* when talking about time. . . 6
    - Using *over* when talking about time. . . 6
    - Using *during* when talking about time. . . 6
    - Using *since* when talking about time. . . 7
    - Using *for* when talking about time. . . 7
    - Using *from* when talking about time. . . 7
    - Using *by* when talking about time. . . 7

    Chapter 1 Practice Session . . . 8

    Chapter 1 Review Session . . . 10

Table of Contents

- **Chapter 2:** Using prepositions to talk about location... 12

    - Using _above_ to talk about place or location... 12
    - Using _across_ to talk about place or location... 12
    - Using _after_ to talk about place or location... 13
    - Using _beside_ to talk about place or location... 13
    - Using _against_ to talk about place / location... 13
    - Using _along_ to talk about place or location... 14
    - Using _among_ to talk about place or location... 14
    - Using _around_ to talk about place or location... 14
    - Using _at_ to talk about place or location... 15
    - Using _in_ to talk about place or location... 15
    - Using _behind_ to talk about place or location... 15
    - Using _on_ to talk about place or location... 16
    - Using _under_, _beneath_, and _below_ when talking about place / location... 16

    Chapter 2 Practice Session... 16

    Chapter 2 Review and Practice Session... 18

Table of Contents

- **Chapter 3:** Using preposition when talking about transportation . . . 21

    - Using *on* when talking about transportation and traveling. 21

    - Using *in into*, and *inside* when talking about transportation and traveling. . . . . 21 - 22

    - Using *by* when talking about transportation and traveling. . . 22

    - Using *off* when talking about transportation and traveling. . . 22

    - Using *between* when talking about transportation and traveling . . . 23

    - Using *from* - to when talking about transportation and traveling . . . 23

    - Using *along* when talking about transportation and traveling . . . 23

    Chapter 3 Practice and Review Session. . . 24

- **Chapter 4:** Using prepositions in sentences giving directions. . . 26

    - Using *towards* to talk about directions . . . 26

    - Using *in* to talk about or giving directions . . . 26

    - Using *on* to talk about or giving directions . . . 27

- Using *near* to talk about or giving directions . . . 27

- Using *across* to talk about directions. . . 27

- Using *at* to talk about or giving directions . . . 28

- Using *around* to talk about or giving directions . . . 28

Chapter 4 Practice and Review Session . . . 29

❏ **Chapter 5:** Practical usage for the prepositions *with* and *by* . . . 31

- Examples of usage: *with* and *by* . . . 31
- Some rules and examples for using the preposition *by* . . . 32
- Some rules and examples for using the preposition *with* . . . 34

Chapter 5 Practice and Review Session . . . 34

Table of Contents

Section 2 ... 38

Using Prepositions correctly after certain common English verbs.

Verbs will be listed in alphabetical order.

❑ **Chapter 1:** Prepositions that follow certain verbs beginning with the letter *A*. . . 39

- absent *from*, 39
- accustomed *to*, 39
- acquainted *with*, 40
- admire *for*, 40
- afraid *of*, 40
- agree *with*, 40
- amazed *at* / *by*, 41
- angry *at* / *with*, 41
- apologize *for* / *to*, 41

- apply *to* / *for*, 42
- approve *of*, 42
- argue *with*, 42
- arrive *at* or *in*, 42
- ashamed *of*, 41
- ask *for* or *about*, 43
- aware *of*, 43
- awful *at*, 43

Chapter 1 Practice and Review. . . 43

xiii

Table of Contents

❑ **Chapter 2:** Prepositions that follow certain verbs beginning with the letter **B** and **C**... 45

- bad *for*, 45
- believe *in*, 45
- belong *to*, 45
- bored with / by, 45
- borrow *from*, 46
- careful *of*, 46
- compare *to* / *with*, 46
- complain *to* / *about*, 46

- composed *of*, 47
- concentrate *on*, 47
- concerned *about*, 47
- consist *of*, 47
- content *with*, 48
- crazy *about*, 48
- curious *about*, 48

Chapter 2 Practice and Review... 49

❑ **Chapter 3:** Prepositions that follow certain verbs beginning with the letter **D** and **E**... 51

- depend *on*, 51
- devoted *to*, 51
- different *from*, 51
- disagree *with*, 52
- disappointed *in*, 52

- discuss *with*, 52
- divide *into*, 52
- divorced *from*, 52
- dream *of*, 53
- engaged *to*, 53

xiv

Table of Contents

- equal *to*, 53
- escape *from*, 53
- excited *about*, 54
- excuse *for*, 54
- exhausted *from*, 54
- familiar *with*, 54

Chapter 3 Practice and Review... 55

❏ **Chapter 4:** Prepositions that follow certain verbs beginning with the letters *F*, *G*, *H*, and *I*... 57

- fond *of*, 57
- forgive *for*, 57
- friendly *with* / *to*, 57
- frightened *of* / *by*, 58
- full *of*, 58
- get rid *of*, 58
- glad *about*, 58
- gone *from*, 59
- good *at*, 58
- good *for*, 59
- graduate *from*, 59
- happen *to*, 59
- hear *about*, 60
- hear *from*, 60
- help *with*, 60
- hide *from*, 60
- hope *for*, 61
- insist *on*, 61
- interested *in*, 61
- introduce *to*, 62
- invite *to*, 62
- involved *in* / *with*, 62

Chapter 4 Practice and Review... 62

Table of Contents

❑ **Chapter 5:** Prepositions that follow certain verbs beginning with the letter _**K**_, _**L**_, and _**M**_ . . . 65

- kind _to_, 65
- know _about_, 65
- laugh _at_, 65
- listen _to_ / _for_, 66
- look _at_ / _for_, 66
- look forward _to_, 66
- mad _at_, 67
- made _for_, 67
- made _of_, 67

- married _to_, 67
- matter _to_, 67
- multiply (this) _by_ (that), 68
- add (this) _to_ (that), 68
- divide (this) _by_ (that), 69
- subtract (this) _from_ (that), 68

Chapter 5 Practice and Review. . . 69

❑ **Chapter 6:** Prepositions that follow certain verbs beginning with the letters _**N**_, _**O**_, _**P**_ and _**Q**_. . . 71

- nervous _about_, 71
- nice _to_, 71
- opposed _to_, 71

- patient _with_, 72
- pay _for_, 72

xvi

Table of Contents

- pleased *with* / *about*, 72
- point *at*, 72
- polite *to*, 72
- prepared *for*, 73

- protect (something / someone) *from*, 73
- proud *of*, 73
- qualified *for*, 73

Chapter 6 Practice and Review... 74

❏ **Chapter 7:** Prepositions that follow certain verbs beginning with the letters *R* and *S*... 76

- ready *for*, 76
- related *to*, 76
- rely *on*, 76
- responsible *for*, 77
- sad *about*, 77
- safe *from*, 77
- satisfied *with*, 78
- scared *of* / *by*, 78
- search *for*, 78
- separate *from*, 78

- sick *of*, 79
- similar *to*, 79
- slow *at*, 79
- sorry *for*, 80
- speak *to* (someone) *about*, 80
- stare *at*, 80
- sure *of*, 81
- surprised *at* / *by*, 79

xvii

Table of Contents

Chapter 7 Practice and Review. . . 81

❑ **Chapter 8:** Prepositions that follow certain verbs beginning with the letters *T* through *Z* . . . 83

- take care *of,* 83
- talk *to* / *with,* 83
- tell *about,* 83
- terrible *at,* 84
- terrified *by* / *of,* 84
- thank *for,* 84
- tired *from,* 84

- tired *of,* 84
- travel *to,* 85
- used *to,* 85
- wait *for,* 85
- wait *on,* 85
- worried *about,* 86

Chapter 8 Practice and Review . . . 86

Section 3 . . . 89

Common English prepositions with explanations and examples in alphabetical order

❑ **Chapter 1:** Common English prepositions with explanations and examples: letters *A* and *B* . . . 90

- about, 90
- above, 91

xviii

Table of Contents

- across, 93
- after, 93
- against, 95
- ahead of, 96
- along, 96
- among, 97
- around, 97
- as, 98
- at, 98

- before, 100
- behind, 101
- below, 101
- beneath, 102
- beside, 102
- besides, 102
- between, 103
- beyond, 105
- by, 106

Chapter 1 Review... 108

- **Chapter 2:** Common English prepositions with explanations and examples: letters *C* through *F*... 110

- close to, 110
- despite, 111
- down, 111
- during, 112

- far from, 112
- for, 113
- from, 115

Chapter 2 Review... 117

Table of Contents

- **Chapter 3:** Common English prepositions with explanations and examples: letters **I** through **N** . . . 120

  - in, 120
  - in back of, 123
  - in front of, 124
  - inside, 124
  - instead of, 124
  - into, 125
  - like, 126
  - near, 127
  - next to, 127

Chapter 3 Review. . . 127

- **Chapter 4:** Common English prepositions with explanations and examples: letter **O** . . . 130

  - of, 130
  - off, 132
  - on, 134
  - onto, 139
  - opposite, 139
  - out, 140
  - outside, 143
  - over, 143

Chapter 4 Review. . . 145

- **Chapter 5:** Common English prepositions with explanations and examples: letters **P** through **T** . . . 148

  - past, 148
  - since, 149

Table of Contents

- through, 149
- throughout, 152
- to, 152
- toward(s), 157

Chapter 5 Review... 159

❏ **Chapter 6:** Common English prepositions with explanations and examples: letters **U** through **Z . . . 161**

- under, 161
- underneath, 162
- until, 163
- up, 163
- upon, 165
- with, 165
- within, 169
- without. 170

Chapter 6 Review... 171

❏ **Appendix:** Prepositions following certain common English verbs, listed by preposition . . .174

Mastering English Prepositions

Section 1: Using Prepositions correctly in context.

Learn to use English prepositions correctly after certain commonly used English verbs.

This first section provides the student with the resources to understand the functional use of English prepositions in real life situations. In this section, the student will find explanations and examples relating to preposition usage in everyday usage.

If the student has the Focus On English audio book that accompanies this text (available separately from the student's school store or from www.FOEBooks.com), then he or she will be able to listen and practice speaking with the many examples that are provided.

Chapter 1

Using the prepositions **_at_**, **_on_**, **_in_**, **_by_**, **_within_**, **_under_**, **_during_**, **_over_**, **_since_**, **_from_**, **_for_** and **_after_** when talking about time in English:

Using prepositions when talking about time

Directions: Read and / or listen to the brief explanations and then the examples below. *(Hint: if you have the Focus On English mp3 audio book for this lesson, it will help you to remember if you repeat the examples along with the teacher.)*

1. Use **_on_** for day names, like Monday or Tuesday.

    Examples:
    - My friends come to visit me **_on_** Wednesday.
    - We have an important exam **_on_** Friday.

2. Use **_on_** in expressions like **_on time_**; **_on time_** means at the correct time or agreed upon time.

    Examples:
    - My boss does not want me to come to work late.
    - He wants me to come to work **_on_** time.

3. Use **_at_** to talk about exact clock time.

    Examples:
    - The exam will start **_at_** 3pm.

- The movie starts *at* 7:15pm.

4. Use *at* to talk about midnight, noon, night, daybreak, sunset, sunrise, etc.

    Examples:
- We had lunch *at* noon.
- We woke up *at* dawn (when the sun comes up).
- We went to bed *at* dusk (when the sun goes down).

5. Use *at* in expressions referring to time: *at* the moment, *at* the present time, etc.

    Examples:
- *At* the moment, doctors are not sure what causes cancer.
- *At* the present time, we are not hiring any more employees.

6. Use *in* to talk about seasons of the year:

    Examples:
- We will start school *in* the fall.
- Our vacation begins *in* the summer

7. Use *in* to talk about centuries, years, and months:

    Examples:

- Cars were invented *in* the nineteenth century.
- We will finish class *in* May.
- We will graduate *in* 2012.

8. Use *in* to talk about blocks of time:
   Example:
   - The woman said that she expects to have children in the future.

9. Use *in* to talk about named times of the day: morning, afternoon, and evening:
   Examples:
   - We have tea *in* the morning.
   - We eat lunch *in* the afternoon.
   - We have dinner *in* the evening.

10. Use *in* to talk about months of the year.
    Example:
    - I will complete my English course *in* February.

11. Use *in* to talk about years.
    Example:
    - I came to this country *in* 2001.

12. Use *in* in expressions like *in* time.
    Example:

- He was just *in time* for dinner. (Meaning: he arrived when dinner was about to be served; at the correct time.)

What is the difference between *in time* and *on time*? *In time* means that something has happened approximately at the same time as something else is happening or about to happen. Example: We are about to have dinner, and you are just *in time* to join us. *On time* means that something has happened exactly at the agreed upon time. Examples: The student was *on time* for school. School begins at 8am. The student was *on time*.

Example:
- He was *in time* for dinner. This means that he arrived at some time near when dinner was being served.

Example:
- We said dinner was at 6pm and he arrived *in time*. This means that he arrived *around* the agreed upon time of 6pm.)

13. Use ***within*** to talk about something happening sometime inside of a specific time frame.
    Example:
    - The bus should arrive *within* the next 15 minutes. (Meaning sometime more than 1 minute and less than 15 minutes. So, for

example, if it is 8pm, the bus should arrive sometime between 8pm and 8:15pm. The bus is not expected to arrive at 8:15pm exactly nor at 8pm exactly, but some time in between these to times.)

14. Use *__under__* when talking about something happening in less than a certain amount of time.
    Example:
    - I'm sure the train will be here in *__under__* an hour. (Meaning in less than an hour)

15. Use *__over__* when talking about something that takes more than a certain amount of time.
    Examples:
    - I have been waiting here for you for *__over__* an hour.
    - The bus took *__over__* an hour to get to its next stop.

16. Use *__during__* to talk about the time span in which something happened.
    Example:
    - She cannot sleep well. She woke up several times *__during__* the night. (The time span was the nighttime hours when she was trying to sleep.)

17. Use *__since__* to talk about situations that began in the past and continue to the present.
    Example:
    - I haven't felt well *__since__* I left my home country. (Use since to refer to a specific time in the past like, for example, 1994 or 2pm.)

18. Use *__for__* to talk about situations that began in the past and continue to the present.
    Examples:
    - I have been waiting here *__for__* the plane for two hours.
    - We have been taking this exam *__for__* 3 hours and I am tired. (Use for to talk about consecutive time like, for example, for 50 minutes or for 20 years.)

19. Use *__from__* to talk about situations that will begin now or began at a certain time and continue into the future.
    Example:
    - Last year we lost a very important soccer match to our rival. We were very sad. *__From__* that time on we never lost another game to our rival.

20. When talking about time, use *__by__* to mean up to a certain time.

8

Example:

- They will finish building our new house *by* next March.

Practice

Directions: Read and / or Listen to the story below. If you are listening to this lesson on an audio book, listen for the prepositions *at*, *on*, *in*, *by*, *within*, *under*, *during*, *over*, *since*, *from*, *for* and *after*. Let's begin:

I won the lottery!

Two weeks ago I won the lottery. I'm going to be rich! My life will change forever.

I've got an appointment with the lottery office *at* 9am *on* Wednesday. I'm going to the lottery office to pick up my $1,000,000 lottery prize.

During the telephone call, the person at the lottery office told me that I had to be at the lottery office *on* January 5th, *at* 9am. That's *on* a Wednesday. I haven't been able to sleep *since* I learned that I won the lottery.

I have been waiting *for* 2 weeks for this appointment. I want to buy many things.

I arrived at the lottery office *at* 8:45am. I was really nervous. The lady at the receptionist desk said that the lottery official would give me my prize money *within* the next 15 minutes. I really hope he'll be here in _**under**_ 10 minutes because I am so excited about receiving this money.

**During** the time that I was waiting, it has been _**over**_ 5 minutes now, I thought about that money. All that money! I was so excited. _**After**_ today, I will be a rich person. I haven't had much money in my life. In fact, I have been poor _**for**_ the last 5 years.

The secretary told me that I was the first person _**in**_ the past 3 years, _**since**_ 2005, to win $1,000,000.

I told her about my dream for the future: "_**by**_ next Wednesday," I said, "I want to have a new car, and _**in**_ 3 years I want to have a home in Fiji."

I told the secretary: "I won't believe I really won the lottery _**until**_ I receive the money in my hands."

Meanwhile, the lottery official opened his door and said, "I'll be out _**in**_ 5 minutes."

I thought to myself: I will buy a brand new car _**by**_ Monday, and, _**by**_ Wednesday, I will buy a new apartment.

In fact, _**by**_ the time you finish listening to this lesson, I will have received my money. The first thing I'm going to do after I get my money is take English lessons!

10

Review: Let's review the use of *on*, *at* and *in* for time sentences

Use *on* for day names, like Monday or Tuesday.

Use *on* in expressions like *on time*.

Use *at* to talk about exact clock time. The exam will start *at* 3pm.

Use *at* to talk about midnight, noon, night, day, etc. For example: we had lunch *at* noon. We woke up *at* dawn. We went to bed *at* dusk (when the sun goes down).

Use *at* in expressions referring to time: *at* the moment, *at* the present time, etc. For example: *At* the moment, we are not sure what causes cancer.

Use *in* to talk about what will or may happen in the future: I will arrive *in* Tokyo *in* 4 days.

Use *in* to talk about seasons of the year. For example: we will start school *in* the fall. Our vacation begins *in* the summer

Use *in* to talk about centuries, years, and months. For example: cars were invented *in* the twentieth century. We will finish class *in* May. We will graduate *in* 2012.

Use *in* to talk about blocks of time. For example: I expect to have children *in* the future.

Use *in* to talk about named times of the day. For example: We have tea *in* the morning. We eat lunch in the afternoon. We have dinner in the evening.

Use *in* to talk about months of the year. For example: I will complete my English course *in* February.

Use *in* to talk about years. For example: I came to this country *in* 2001.

Use *in* in expressions like: *in* time. For example: He was just *in time* for dinner.

Snapshot

What is the difference between *in time* and *on time*? *In time* means that something has happened approximately at the correct time. *On time* means that something has happened exactly at the right time.

He was *in time* for dinner. Means that he arrived at some time just before dinner was being served.

We said dinner was at 6pm and he arrived *on time*. Means that he arrived exactly at 6pm.

Chapter 2

Using the prepositions *above*, *across*, *after*, *against*, *along*, *among*, *around*, *at*, *below*, *beside*, *between*, *beneath*, *from*, *in*, *off*, *on*, *under*, and *towards* when talking about place or location:

Using prepositions when talking about place or location:

1. When talking about place, use ***above*** to mean something that is higher up than something else.
    Examples:
    - Oh look at that beautiful bird flying *above* our heads.
    - The president is *above* all other managers in the company.
    - The ceiling is *above* the floor.

2. When talking about place, use ***across*** to express: from one side to the other.
    Examples:
    - The chicken walked *across* the street to eat some corn.
    - The chicken walked *across* the busy street safely.

- The cruise ship sailed *across* the ocean to Europe.
- The man walked *across* the bridge to visit his secret lover.

3. Use *after* when talking about the 'next one' when talking about place or location.

   Examples:
   - The food store is the next building *after* the bank.
   - The shopping mall is located on the next block *after* the high school.

4. Use *beside* when talking about something that is at the side of or next to something or someone.

   Examples:
   - The clothing store is *beside* the bank.
   - The student sat *beside* the teacher while the teacher corrected his exam.

5. When talking about place or location, *against* means something contacting or touching something else, pressing on it or pushing on it.

   Examples:
   - The woman leaned *against* the wall waiting for her boyfriend to meet her.
   - The traffic was so bad that cars were almost *against* one another.

6. *Along* means over the length of something.
   Example:
   - The man walked *along* the busy road on his way to work.

7. *Among* means something or someone in a group of people or things. There are usually more than two people or things in the group.
   Example:
   - The woman walked in the park *among* the flowers and trees. Compare: She walked *between* two tall trees.

8. *Around*, meaning 1: means in the immediate vicinity. Another way to say this is something that is approximately close by or near.
   Example:
   - The new hotel is *around* here, but we are not exactly sure where.

9. *Around*, meaning 2: when we talk about a place being on the other side of something (sometimes obscured from your view by something).
   Examples:
   - The bank is *around* the corner from here.
   - The police station is *around* the other side of the building.

10. *Around*, meaning 3: moving here and there, randomly.

Examples:
- The couple walked *around* the neighborhood.
- The boy rode his bicycle *around* the town.

11. Use *at* to express being in front of, or up to something, but not in it.

    Example:
    - He arrived *at* the train station *at* 3pm. Compare this with: He went *into* the train station after he arrived.
    - He was *in* the train station for 2 hours before his train arrived. The train took him to the airport.
    - He was *at* the airport by 6pm. He went *into* the airport to get his ticket. He was *in* the airport for 3 hours before his flight.
    - The trash is kept *at* the back of the airport building.

12. Use *in* to talk about your location within a city, state, country or other named political area.

    Examples:
    - I will arrive *in* Tokyo in 4 days. (Not *at* Tokyo)
    - He arrived *in* New York on Wednesday.

13. *Behind* means at the back of or the rear of something or someone.

    Examples:

- The trash is kept *behind* the building.
- The boy watched the house burn while his little sister hid *behind* him.

14. Use *on* to talk about something in contact with or over a surface.
    Examples:
    - The book is *on* top of the desk.
    - The book is *on* the desk.
    - The picture is *on* the wall.
    - The clock is *on* the wall.
    - The map is *on* the wall.
    - The light is *on* the ceiling.

15. You can use *under*, *beneath* and *below* in similar ways when you want to express something being physically lower than something else.
    Examples:
    - His feet are *under* the desk.
    - His feet are *beneath* the desk.
    - His feet are *below* the desk.

Practice

Directions: Read and / or listen to this brief story about an college student named Tommy Morgan and his friends and see if you can hear how the following prepositions are used:

above, *across*, *after*, *against*, *along*, *among*, *around*, *at*, *below*, *beside*, *between*, *beneath*, *from*, *in*, *off*, *on*, *under*, and *towards*. After reading and / or listening you will be given some individual example sentences to practice with.

Tommy Morgan and His Friends

Tommy Morgan sits *in* his chair *at* his desk. *On* his desk there is a book. *In* the drawer *in* his desk, there are some school supplies like, for example, pencils and pens. His feet are *on* the floor *below* the desk and his hands are *above* the desk while his elbows rest *on* the desk.

His pen is *between* the pages of his book. His book is *on* his desk. His favorite pen is *among* the school supplies *inside* the drawer *in* his desk. His desk is located *in* the middle *of* the room.

Tommy Morgan wears very nice shoes *on* his feet. *In* his right hand there is a pencil. His teacher sometimes tells him he should take his hat off. So he takes his hat off and puts it *under* the chair where he sits. His friend Mary sits in front of him *at* her desk. His friend Hiro sits *at* the desk *at* the back of the room. His friend Julio sits *at* the desk *behind* Tommy.

Today, the teacher is talking to the students about English grammar. *At* the top *of* the whiteboard, the teacher wrote three irregular verbs. *At* the bottom *of* the whiteboard the teacher wrote three regular verbs. The teacher asks Tommy to come *to* the white board and write a sentence for each verb. She asks him to write the sentences *in* the middle of the whiteboard. Tommy leaned *against* the whiteboard and thought for a moment. Then he began to write his sentences *in* the middle of the whiteboard.

Across from the university, there is a pub. The pub is *on* the corner of Warren Avenue and Jackson Place. *On* Friday nights, Tommy, Hiro, Julio and Mary meet *at* the pub. Mary asked Hiro, "where is the new restaurant that you told me about?' Hiro answered, "I'm not sure, I read about it in the newspaper; it's *around* here, not too far away." Mary replied, "oh, so the restaurant is near the pub. Let's go to the restaurant after we go to the pub."

Inside the pub everyone was having a great time. They went *into* the pub and had such a good time that they stayed there for four hours and forgot their idea about going to the restaurant!

Review and Practice:

*Directions: Read and / or listen carefully to the sentences below. Fill in the blanks using one of the following prepositions: **above**, **across**, **after**, **against**, **along**, **among**, **around**, **at**, **below**, **beside**, **between**, **beneath**, **from**, **in**, **off**, **on**, **under**, and **towards**. The answers can be found in this chapter (above).*

1. Oh look at that beautiful bird flying _____ our heads.

2. The ceiling is _____ our heads.

3. The man walked _____ the street to visit his secret lover.

4. Wal-Mart is the next building _____ the bank.

5. Wal-Mart is _____ the bank.

6. The woman leaned _____ the wall waiting for her boyfriend to meet her.

7. The man walked _____ the busy road on his way to work.

8. The woman walked ___ the park among the flowers and trees.

9. The new hotel is _____ here, but we are not exactly sure where.

10. The couple walked _____ the neighborhood.

11. He arrived ___ the train station at 3pm.

12. He arrived ___ New York *on* Wednesday.

13. The businesswoman is *in* the car. The man got ____ the train and then ____ a plane to New York.

14. We arrived *at* the train station ____ 2pm. Then we went inside the train station. We were *in* the train station _____ our train arrived ___ 3pm.

15. The chicken walked _____ the busy street safely.

16. The trash is kept _____ the building.

17. The trash is kept ___ the back *of* the building.

18. The book is ___ top *of* the desk. The book is <u>*on*</u> the desk

19. His feet are _____ the desk. His feet are beneath the desk. His feet are below the desk.

Chapter 3

Using the prepositions *in*, *on*, *at*, *into*, *off*, *across*, *from* - *to*, *along* and *between* when talking about transportation and traveling:

Using prepositions when talking about transportation and traveling

Use *on* to talk about trains, buses, and planes. *(Contrast with in.)*

Examples:

- I got *on* the bus to go to the center of the city.
- When we got *on* the plane, we had a difficult time finding our seats.
- We got *on* the train just in time; the train was about to leave.
- The man got *on* the train and then *on* a plane to New York.

Note: it *is* true that you are inside the bus, train or plane when you are traveling, but English speakers say "I'm *on* a bus to Seattle", for example, if someone calls them on their cell phone. It is more common for English speakers to use *in* or *inside* when talking about public transportation when they are talking about things that may have happened while they were traveling, or things that were observed inside the transportation vehicle.

Examples:
- There was a lot of noise *inside* the bus while we were going home.
- All of the passengers *in* the plane were enjoying the movie.
- The lights *in* the train were very low.

1. Use *in* and *into* to talk about taxis, cars and limousines.
   Examples:
   - The businesswoman left her house at 10pm and then got *into* her car and drove to work.
   - The two students waved at the taxi to stop.
   - When the taxi stopped, they got *in* and told the taxi driver where they wanted to go.

2. Use *by* to talk about how you traveled; what form of transportation.
   Examples:
   - The family traveled by plane to Beijing.
   - The boy went to school by foot.
   - The businesswoman traveled to Frankfurt by train.
   - We went to the movies by bike.

3. Use *off* in the phrasal verb, **_to get off_**, to talk about disembarking and arriving at a destination.
   Examples:
   - The businessman took the train to New Jersey and *got off* in Newark.
   - We are taking a plane to Dallas but we are *getting off* in Reno, Nevada.

   (Note: Don't use *get off* when referring to a taxi, car, or limousine. Use *get out of* or *arrived in* a taxi, car or limousine. For example: I arrived in New York *in* a taxi. I *got out*, paid the taxi driver, and went *inside* the train station to catch the next train to Philadelphia.)

4. Use **_between_** to talk about distance from one location to another location.
   Example:
   - What is the distance *between* New York and Los Angeles? Oh, it's about 2400 miles.

5. Use **_from - to_** to talk about travel plans or distance *from* one location *to* another location.
   Example:
   - How long does it take to travel *from* New York *to* Chicago?
   - The distance *from* Seattle, Washington *to* Atlanta,
   - Georgia is about 2,900 miles.

- Could you tell me how to get *to* St. Peters Cathedral *from* here.

6. Use ***along*** to talk about traveling over a length of road or train track.
   Example:
   - We took a train to Miami, Florida.
   - As we traveled *along* the tracks, we could see many farms.

Practice and Review

Directions: Read and / or listen to this brief story about an English student named Sonya as she travels for the first time in the United States. Read and / or listen carefully to how prepositions are used to talk about transportation and traveling. Fill in the blanks with the correct preposition.

Sonya's first trip to Seattle

Sonya came to the U.S. last year to study English ____ New York. She arrived *in* New York ____ May 30th. After studying English *in* New York, she decided to travel *across* the United States using ground transportation like trains, buses, and taxis so that she could see what America looked like.

____ New York, she decided to take a train *to* Cleveland, Ohio. On the day that she decided to leave, she got ____ a taxi in front of her hotel and told the driver to take her to the railroad station. When she arrived *at* the railroad station she got _out_ of the taxi, paid the driver, and went _____ the train station.

After she bought her ticket _at_ the ticket counter, she waited _inside_ the train station for over an hour, until her train arrived.

When the train arrived and opened its doors, Sonya got _____ the train and found a nice seat _by_ the window.

She took many pictures _from_ her window seat during the ride to Cleveland. The train was scheduled to stop ___ Pittsburgh, Pennsylvania and Alliance, Ohio before continuing on to Cleveland. When the train stopped _in_ Pittsburgh, Sonya got _____ to have a quick look around.

After getting ___ the train again, Sonya had some dinner. As the train traveled _along_ the tracks, the sun was going down. Sonya is going to arrive in Cleveland at dusk, just in time to find a hotel room for the evening.

Chapter 4

Using the prepositions *__in__*, *__on__*, *__at__*, *__near__*, *__down__*, *__towards__*, *__across__*, *__from__*, *__between__*, *__around__* and *__among__* when talking about giving directions:

Using prepositions when giving directions

1. When giving directions, use *towards* to mean in the direction of something.

   Example:
   - Could you please tell me how to get to the bank?
   - Sure. Walk down this street *__towards__* the fountain in the center of the city. Turn left at Warner Street.

2. When giving directions, use *__in__* to mean inside of an area or boundary.

   Example:
   - Could you please tell me how to get to the bank?
   - Sure. Walk down this street towards the fountain *__in__* the center of the city. Turn left at Warner Street and you will see the bank on your right, *__in__* the financial district.

3. When giving directions, use *on* with street, road or highway to indicate location; or use *on* in expressions like *on the right*.

   Example:
   - Could you please tell me how to get to the bank?
   - Sure. Walk down this street towards the fountain in the center of the city. Turn left at Warner Street and you will see the bank *on* your right, in the financial district. It's *on* Warner Street near Sunrise Road.

4. When giving directions, use *near* to mean close to.

   Example:
   - Could you please tell me how to get to the bank?
   - Sure. Walk down this street towards the fountain in the center of the city. Turn left at Warner Street and you will see the bank on your right, in the financial district. It's on Warner Street *near* Sunrise Road.

5. When giving directions, use *across* to mean from one side to the other side.

   Example:
   - Could you please tell me how to get to the bank?

- Sure. Walk down this street towards the fountain in the center of the city. Turn left at Warner Street and you will see the bank on your right, in the financial district. It's on Warner Street near Sunrise Road. You may need to walk _across_ the street. It's _across_ from the library and between the food store and the computer store.

6. When giving directions, use **_at_** to indicate the location of something.

    Example:
    - Could you please tell me how to get to the bank?
    - Sure. From here, walk down this street towards the fountain in the center of the city. Turn left _at_ Warner Street and you will see the bank on your right, in the financial district. It's on Warner Street near Sunrise Road. You may need to walk across the street. It's across from the library and between the food store and the computer store. There are some trees growing _at_ the front of the bank building. The bank is around the corner from the new park.

7. When giving directions, use **_around_** to talk about something being close, or something located on the other side of something else.

Example:
- Could you please tell me how to get to the bank?
- Sure. From here, walk down this street towards the fountain in the center of the city. Turn left at Warner Street and you will see the bank on your right, in the financial district. It's on Warner Street near Sunrise Road. You may need to walk across the street. It's across from the library and between the food store and the computer store. There are some trees growing at the front of the bank building. The bank is _around_ the corner from the new park, _around_ where the library is.

Practice and Review:

Let's read and / or listen again to the discussion about finding the bank. Pay attention to the prepositions and how they are used. See if you can fill in the blanks with the correct answers.

Could you please tell me how to get to the bank? Sure. _From_ here, walk _down_ this street _towards_ the fountain ___ the center _of_ the city. Turn left ___ Warner Street and you will see the bank _on_ your right, _in_ the financial district. It's _on_ Warner Street _near_ Sunrise Road. You may need to walk _____ the street. It's _across_ _from_ the library and _between_ the food store and the computer store. There are some trees growing *at* the front of the bank building. The bank is _____ the corner *from* the new park, *around* where the library is.

Chapter 5

Using **_with_** and **_by_** to express how things are done.

Using _with_ and _by_ to express how things are done

Below we will discuss these important prepositions and provide you with many examples. If you have the Focus On English audio book that goes with this lesson, listen carefully to the pronunciation of these expressions in complete sentences.

Examples:

1. The beautiful dress was made _by_ hand. Katrina made the beautiful dress _with_ her own hands.

2. The construction worker dug the hole _by_ hand (meaning: manually, with a shovel in his hands; without the help of a machine). The construction worker dug the hole _with_ his hands (meaning manually, without a shovel or the help of a machine; literally with his two hands).

3. The family traveled to South Africa _by_ air. We sent the letter _by_ airmail. We went to school every day _by_ foot.

4. We walked into the wrong room _by_ mistake.

5. We paid for the meal *with* a check. We paid for the meal *by* check. We paid for the meal *in cash*.

6. We were lucky; *by* chance we found the examination room right before the exam was going to begin.

Some rules and examples for using *with* and *by*:

1. ***By*** is used to talk about the way you travel or how you travel.
    For example:
    - I go to work *by* bus. I went to Europe *by* plane.

2. ***By*** is used to talk about how you communicate or send mail or packages.
    For example:
    - We talked *by* phone.
    - We sent the package to India *by* airmail.
    - My friend and I communicate *by* email.

3. ***By*** is also used in expressions like:
    - ***By mistake*** (meaning: to do something in error);
        Example:
        - I dialed the wrong number *by mistake*. I apologized to the person who answered the phone.
    - ***By check*** (meaning: a method of payment).
        Example:

- I often pay my bills *by check*.

Note: if you pay for something with cash, we often say '*in cash*'.
Examples:
- I paid for the new car *in* cash.
- I paid the bill *in* cash.

It is also possible to say *with cash*.
Example:
- I paid for the tickets *with cash*.

- ***By chance*** (not planned; luckily or unluckily).
  Example:
  - *By* chance, the dress was on sale when we arrived at the shop. We didn't expect to find the dress on sale.

- ***By choice***.
  Example:
  - *By* choice, I am single (not married) (meaning I choose not to be married).

- Using ***by + a gerund***. Use *by* + a *gerund* to express doing something.
  Example:

- I sent an email _**by**_ press_**ing**_ the send button.
- I repaired the car _**by**_ adjust_**ing**_ the engine.

4. Use _**with**_ when you are talking about doing something _**with**_ a tool or an instrument or when you are talking about doing something _**with**_ some part of your body.

   Examples:
   - I fixed the engine _**with**_ a wrench.
   - I kicked the door _**with**_ my foot.
   - I sewed the clothing _**with**_ a needle

Let's practice and review:

Read and / or listen to the following story and fill in the blanks with either _**by**_ or _**with**_. Answers can be found in this chapter (above).

1. My friend Jaime and I decided to travel to Hawaii for our vacation. We knew that the flight ____ plane was going to be a long one from Europe, but we really wanted to go to Hawaii.

2. Before we bought tickets, we decided to contact our travel agent in Barcelona ____ email to get more information about travel to Hawaii. By chance, out travel agent was working ____ her computer when

our email arrived, and she answered our email quickly.

3. She answered our email ____ telling us that she would be happy to give us a brochure about travel to Hawaii. She said that it was probably a good idea to bring a credit card because paying for everything ____ cash was not practical, and it would be dangerous to walk around ____ lots of cash in our pockets. Paying ____ personal check was not a good idea either because many stores in Hawaii do not accept checks that are not from a local bank in Hawaii. She said that going to Hawaii ____ Traveler's Checks was a good idea because merchants accepted these in the same way that they accept cash and they were safe to carry in our pockets.

4. When we arrived in Hawaii, we traveled ____ bus from the airport to our hotel room. During the ride from the airport we could see Hawaii's beautiful beaches and parks. It smelled like the air was filled ____ flowers, and it was warm and the sky was very blue.

5. The bus let us off in front of a group of hotels ____ all of our luggage. ____ mistake, we walked into the wrong hotel. When we asked the clerk at the desk about our reservation, the clerk said that our names were not on the list.

6. ___ chance, there was another person standing at the counter who offered to help. He looked at our itinerary and quickly helped us to find our hotel, which was right next door. He walked with us a little so he could point to the hotel.

7. After getting settled in our hotel room, the rest of the vacation in Hawaii was very exciting. We went ___ bus to see the island.

Mastering English Prepositions

Section 2: *Using Prepositions correctly after certain common English verbs.*

Learn to use English prepositions correctly after certain commonly used English verbs.

English has many important expressions that use a combination of verbs plus prepositions or adjectives (beginning with the "be" verb) plus prepositions.

How do you know which preposition to use after these verbs? Well, there are no set rules for this. But don't worry! This Focus On English section will help you to understand and then practice and master using these verb- preposition combinations correctly.

If you have the Focus On English audio book that accompanies this text (available separately from your school store or from www.FOEBooks.com), then you will be able to listen and practice speaking with the many examples that are provided.

Chapter 1
*Prepositions following verbs beginning with **A***

There are no set rules that might help you to understand which preposition follows a variety of common English verbs. So here you will find the English verbs that are commonly followed by prepositions. Verb / preposition combinations are followed by some examples of how English speakers typically use these in a wide variety of English sentences.

If you have the Focus On English audio book that accompanies this lesson (available separately from your school store or from www.FOEBooks.com), each example will be spoken twice.

Using prepositions in expressions with certain verbs - Verbs beginning with the letter A

To ***be absent from***:
   Examples:
   - Students should not ***be absent from*** class.
   - Alex ***was*** not ***absent from*** the meeting.

To ***be accustomed to*** (something or someone) (similar in meaning to be used to):
   Examples:
   - The girl ***is accustomed to*** shopping at the store near her house.

- Kaori *is accustomed to* walking home from school.

To *be acquainted with* (something or someone):
Examples:
- I *am acquainted with* that man. He is the one who brought the package to our house.
- We *were acquainted with* the school's rules because we went to an orientation.

To *admire for* (something or someone):
Examples:
- I *admire him for* getting a high grade on his exam.
- Gina *admired her mother for* getting a university degree.

To be *afraid of* (something or someone):
Examples: I *am afraid of* walking home alone in the dark.
Lucy *is afraid of* swimming in the ocean.

To *agree with* (something or someone)
Examples:
- I *agree with* my friend. We both have the same opinion about politics.
- Sally *agreed with* her advisor when her advisor told her she should change jobs.

To be _ashamed of_ (something or someone)
   Examples:
   - I _am ashamed of_ my friend for stealing the car.
   - Clarence _was ashamed of_ the bad grade that he got on the exam.

To be _amazed at_ or _by_ (something or someone)
   Examples:
   - I _am amazed at_ how hard he studied for that exam; almost 5 hours every night!
   - The crowd _was amazed at_ the circus act.

To be _angry at_ or _with_ (something or someone)
   Examples:
   - I _am angry with_ / _at_ my girlfriend for not telling me she was dating someone else.
   - The tourists were angry _with_ / _at_ the tour guide for speaking too quickly.

To _apologize for_ (doing something wrong) or _to_ (something or someone)
   Examples:
   - I _apologized_ to the teacher _for_ being late. I _apologized for_ being late.

- The policeman *apologized* to his boss *for* arresting the wrong person.

To *apply to* or *for*
Examples:
- I *applied to* the school for admission. I *applied for* admission.
- Sam *applied for* a new job.

To *approve of* (something or someone)
Examples:
- My company *approves of* the way I dress when I come to work.
- The passengers on the plane *approved of* the way the stewardess did her job.

To *argue with* (something or someone)
Examples:
- I *argued with* my boss about the project deadline.
- She *argued with* her mother about staying out past 10pm.

To *arrive at* or *in* (*at* a location / building; *in* a city or country)
Examples:
- I *arrived at* school at 8am. She will *arrive in* the United States on Wednesday.

- The hockey team *arrived at* the arena at 4:30pm.

To *ask for* or *about* (something or someone)
Examples:
- I *asked* him *for* a pencil.
- I *asked* her *about* the exam that she took yesterday.
- The little boy *asked* his grandpa *for* some candy.

To be *aware of* (something or someone)
Examples:
- He *is aware of* the penalty for breaking the law.
- We *were aware of* the high prices before we entered the store.

To be *awful at* (something or someone)
Examples:
- He *is awful at* cooking. It's lucky that he has a wife that can cook.
- She *is awful at* drawing pictures. She's better at writing.

Let's practice and review:

Read and / or listen to the following story and fill in the blanks with the correct preposition. Answers can be found in this chapter (above).

1. Our boss *approves* ____ the way we completed the report.

2. James *asked* his teacher _____ the exam yesterday.

3. My friend *agrees* _____ me.

4. I *am ashamed* _____ our team for losing so badly.

5. I *admire him* ____ being brave during the match.

6. Sally *is afraid* ____ walking home alone in the dark.

7. Tricia *is accustomed* _____ riding the bus home from school.

8. Four students were *absent* ____ school.

9. Jim *was angry* _____ his girlfriend for not telling him that she was dating someone else.

10. The tourists *were amazed* _____ how big the building was.

11. The student *applied* ___ the school for admission.

12. I *apologized* to the bus driver *for* my extra baggage.

13. Jackie argued _____ her boss about the new project.

Chapter 2

*Prepositions following verbs beginning with **B** and **C***

Using prepositions in expressions with certain verbs - B and C

If you have the Focus On English audio book that accompanies this lesson (available from your school store or from FOEBooks.com), listen carefully to the pronunciation of these expressions in sentences.

To be *bad for* (something or someone)
   Examples:
   - Smoking *is bad for* your health.
   - Factory pollution *is bad for* the environment.

To *believe in* (something or someone)
   Examples:
   - I *believe in* good luck.
   - The people *believed in* its government.

To *belong to* (something or someone)
   Examples:
   - The pen *belongs to* me.
   - The sports car *belongs to* the movie star.

To be *bored with* or *by* (something or someone)

Examples:
- I'm *bored with* working every day.
- I'm *bored by* that TV show. Can we change the channel?

To *borrow* something *from* (something or someone)
Examples:
- Tommy Twoshoes *borrowed* $10 *from* Julio. (By the way: Julio lent $10 to Tommy Twoshoes)
- Alicia *borrowed* Jim's bicycle *from* him.

To be *careful of* (something or someone)
Examples:
- *Be careful of* the fast-moving cars when you cross the street!
- Calvin told me to *be careful of* drinking tap water when traveling.

To *compare to* or *with* (something or someone)
Examples:
- When I *compare* swimming *with* (*to*) running, I think that swimming is more difficult.
- *Compared to* our team, the opponent's team looks weak.

To *complain to* or *about*(about something or someone)

Examples:

- I *complained to* my teacher *about* the cold air conditioning in the room.
- Ginger *complained about* the bad food in the restaurant.

To be *composed of* (something)
Examples:
- Coke a Cola *is composed of* (made of) mostly sugar.
- Bread *is composed of* mostly flour.

To *concentrate on* (something or someone)
Examples:
- The student has an exam the next day so he *concentrated on* studying.
- The athlete *concentrates on* winning.

To be *concerned about* (something or someone)
Example:
- She *is concerned about* her weight. She is gaining weight.
- His parents *were concerned about* his poor grades in school.

To *consist of* (something) (meaning: made up of certain ingredients)

Examples:
- A good meal *consists of* fish, vegetables and rice.
- A good report *consists of* lots of research and hard work.

To be *content with* (something or someone) (meaning: to be happy with)
Examples:
- The quiet, simple man *is content with* his life.
- Amy *is content with* her new car.

To be *crazy about* (something or someone)
Example:
- She *is crazy about* ice cream. She really likes to eat ice cream.
- She'*s crazy about* her boyfriend.

To be *curious about* (something or someone)
Examples:
- The customer *was curious about* the price of the car.
- The police detective was curious about the blood on the floor.

Let's practice and review:

Read and / or listen to the following story and fill in the blanks with the correct preposition. Answers can be found in this chapter (above).

1. The red Ferrari *belongs* _____ me.

2. Fiberglass *is composed* _____ silica fibers.

3. The student *was curious* _____ the cost of the textbook.

4. Good Italian pasta sauce *consists* _____ tomatoes, garlic, olive oil, and seasoning.

5. His father *was concerned* _____ the cost of a new roof for his house.

6. The children *believe* _____ magic.

7. Drinking too much alcohol *is bad* _____ your health.

8. Tim Evans *borrowed* $20 _____ Hiro.

9. *Be careful* ____ the snake on the ground right next to you!

10. Jenny *complained* _____ her teacher _____ the noise in the next room.

11. My friend *compared* his car _____ mine and decided to buy a new car.

12. The swim team _concentrated_ _____ learning better techniques.

Chapter 3
*Prepositions following verbs beginning with **D** and **E***

Using prepositions in expressions with certain verbs - D and E

If you have the Focus On English audio book that accompanies this lesson (available from your school store), listen carefully to the pronunciation of these expressions in sentences.

To **_depend on_** (something or someone)
> **Examples:**
> - Car motors **_depend on_** gasoline or diesel fuel to run.
> - She **_depends on_** her friends for help with her homework.

To be **_devoted to_** (something or someone; to be loyal to)
> **Examples:**
> - She *is devoted to* her husband.
> - The professor *is devoted to* his research.

To be **_different from_** (something or someone)
> **Examples:**
> - Coffee *is different from* tea.
> - Apples *are different from* oranges.

To **_disagree with_** (something or someone)
   Examples:
   - I *disagreed with* him about smoking in the classroom.
   - The lawyers *disagreed with* each other in court.

To be **_disappointed in_** (something or someone)
   Examples:
   - I *was disappointed in* our team. They lost the game.
   - Jenny *was disappointed in* the quality of the fruit at the market.

To **_discuss_** (something) **_with_** (someone)
   Examples:
   - I *discussed* the problem *with* my boss.
   - The students *discussed* the assignment *with* the teacher.

To **_divide into_** (divide something into)
   Examples:
   - I *divided* the cake *into* two pieces so my friend could have some.
   - The manager *divided* the workers *into* three groups.

To be **_divorced from_** (something or someone)
   Examples:

- The woman *was divorced from* her husband.
- They *have been divorced from* each other for two years.

To *dream of* (something or someone)
   Examples:
- She *dreamed of* going to the South Pacific for a vacation.
- The couple *dreamed of* having their own house in the future.

To be *engaged to* (someone)
   Examples:
- The man and woman *were engaged to* each other. They planned to get married in one month.
- Alex and Cynthia *were engaged to* each other in March, but broke off the engagement in April.

To be *equal to* (something or someone)
   Examples:
- His English skills *are equal to* her English skills.
- The two soccer teams *are equal to* each other in match records.

To *escape from* (something or someone)
   Examples:

- The prisoner *escaped from* prison and the police cannot find him.
- The young dog *escaped from* the cage and ran away.

To be *excited about* (something or someone)
Examples:
- I *am excited about* my summer vacation. I am going to Asia.
- We *are excited about* going to Hawaii.

To *excuse* (someone) *for*:
Examples:
- My boss *excused* me *for* being late for work.
- Frank *excused* his friend *for* not wanting to go on the hike.

To be *exhausted from* (something)
Examples:
- I *was exhausted from* working in the garden all day.
- Our team *was exhausted from* playing so hard in the competition.

To be *familiar with* (something)
Examples:
- I *am familiar with* the laws in my country (meaning: I know what the laws are in my country).

- Jackie spent two years in Los Angeles and was very *familiar with* that city.

Let's practice and review:

Read and / or listen to the following story and fill in the blanks with the correct preposition. Answers can be found in this chapter (above).

1. I *divided* the cake _____ five pieces so all of my friends could have some.

2. Our team lost. I *was* really *disappointed* _____ our team.

3. We *discussed* the plan _____ our superior.

4. The players *disagreed* _____ the referee.

5. Monty *is devoted* _____ playing the violin.

6. Airline pilots *depend* _____ ground control to help them land safely.

7. Surfing *is different* _____ snow boarding.

8. My brother *dreamed* _____ becoming an engineer.

9. Toby's grades *are equal* _____ the best grades in the school.

10. We are in love. My girlfriend and I *are engaged* ____ each other.

11. The gorilla *escaped* ____ its cage and is now somewhere in the city.

12. The child *was excited* ____ going to the zoo.

13. The workers *were exhausted* ____ working in the sun all day.

14. He *was familiar* ____ the design of the engine.

Chapter 4
*Prepositions following verbs beginning with **F**, **G**, **H**, and **I***

Using prepositions in expressions with certain verbs - F, G, H, and I

If you have the Focus On English audio book that accompanies this lesson (available from your school store), listen carefully to the pronunciation of these expressions in sentences.

To *forgive* (someone) *for* (something)
Examples:
- I *forgive* you *for* coming late.
- Rodney *forgave* the barber *for* the bad haircut.

To be *fond of* (something)
Examples:
- I *am fond of* Italian food. I eat it almost every night.
- Sarah *is* very *fond of* her boyfriend.

To be *friendly with / to* (someone)
Examples:
- The people of New Zealand *are* very *friendly to* foreigners.
- The woman who works at the pub *is* very *friendly with* the customers.

To be *frightened of / by* (something)
>   **Examples:**
>   - I *am frightened of* the dark.
>   - She *is frightened by* his behavior.

To be *full of* (something)
>   **Examples:**
- The car *is full of* gas.
- The arena *is full of* people.

To *get rid of* (something)
>   **Examples:**
- I am going to *get rid of* my old pants because they have too many holes in them.
- The company president wants to *get rid of* employees who are not working hard.

To be *glad about* (somewhere)
>   **Examples:**
- Your team just won the game! Wow, I*'m glad about* that.
- Kathy *was glad about* finishing school.

To be *good at* (something)
>   **Examples:**
- He*'s good at* speaking English.

- Mr. Frankel *is good at* teaching English.

To be *good for* (something)
Examples:
- That hammer *is good for* pounding nails into wood
- Yoga *is good for* your health.

To be *gone from* (somewhere)
Examples:
- I'll *be gone from* the office for two hours.
- Hiromi *was gone from* school for a week because of illness.

To *graduate from* (somewhere)
Examples:
- She *graduated from* university last year with a degree in mathematics.
- John and I *graduated from* high school last year.

To *happen to* (do something)
Examples:
- When you were in school, did you *happen to* see your friend, Kazu? (*Happen to* means 'by chance').
- When Joy was at the mall she *happened to* see her friend Alice.

To be *happy about* (something)
  Examples:
  - The student *was* very *happy about* getting an A on the exam.
  - The shopkeeper *was happy about* all the customers that came to his store.

To *hear about* (something)
  Examples:
  - Did you *hear about* the bank robbery yesterday?
  - We *heard about* the cancellation of the concert and we were not happy.

To *hear from* (someone)
  Examples:
  - She *heard from* her good friend in Japan. She got an email from her yesterday.
  - I haven't *heard from* my brother in six months. I hope he's okay.

To *help* (someone) *with* (something)
  Examples:
  - I will *help* you *with* your homework.
  - The clerk *helped* me *with* filling out the form.

To *hide* (something) *from* (someone)

Examples:
- He *hid* her birthday gift *from* her until the day of her birthday.
- The boy *hid from* his friend in order to surprise him when he arrived.

To *hope for* (something)
Examples:
- We *are hoping for* nice weather tomorrow because we want to have a picnic.
- The students who didn't study were *hoping for* an easy exam.

To *insist on* (something)
Examples:
- Because it was dark, the kind taxi driver *insisted on* walking us to our door.
- The young man *insisted on* driving the car before buying it.

To be *interested in* (something or someone)
Examples:
- The business student *is interested in* learning to speak English well.
- My sister and I *are interested in* investing in real estate.

To *__introduce__* (someone) *__to__* (someone)
> **Examples:**
> - I would like to *__introduce__* you *__to__* my friend, Stephan.
> - Stefan *__introduced__* his friend *__to__* me.

To *__invite__* (someone) *__to__* (something)
> **Examples:**
> - I would like to *__invite__* you *__to__* my party.
> - Shawn was *__invited__* *__to__* William's party.

To be *__involved in__* (something) with (someone)
> **Examples:**
> - We are working together to finish this school project; we *__are involved in__* this school project.
> - The beautiful lady *__is involved with__* the prince of England. (Meaning: she is having a relationship with the prince.)

Let's practice and review:

Read and / or listen to the following story and fill in the blanks with the correct preposition. Answers can be found in this chapter (above).

1. She'*__s good__* _____ English grammar.

2. My friend Bill is going to *get rid* ____ his old pants because they have too many holes in them.

3. Gene *is frightened* ____ lizards.

4. You just won the lottery! Wow, I am sure you *are glad* _____ that.

5. Brad *graduated* _____ English school last year and can now speak English very well.

6. The boss *will be gone* _____ the office for a day.

7. When you were shopping, did you *happen* ____ see your friend, Aiko?

8. Janet *was* very *happy* _____ getting a passing grade on the exam.

9. Did you *hear* _____ the terrible explosion yesterday?

10. The doorman *insisted* ____ carrying our luggage.

11. Jeff *hid* his girlfriend's birthday gift _____ her until the day of her graduation.

12. Claudia *is interested* ____ learning to speak English well.

13. The boss wants to *invite* you ____ the company party.

14. Four of us *are involved* ____ the community project.

15. I would like to *introduce* you ____ my friend, Frank.

Chapter 5
*Prepositions following verbs beginning with **K**, **L**, and **M***

Using prepositions in expressions with certain verbs - K, L, and M

If you have the Focus On English audio book that accompanies this lesson (available from your school store), listen carefully to the pronunciation of these expressions in sentences.

To be **_kind to_** (someone)
    Examples:
- The young boy **_was_** very **_kind to_** the old lady and helped her to walk across the busy street.

The clerk in the candy store **_was_** always **_kind to_** children. He gave them a free piece of candy when they came into the store.

To **_know about_** (something)
    Examples:
- The students didn't **_know about_** the test that the teacher planned for next Tuesday.
- We were new students and didn't **_know about_** the rules in the school.

To **_laugh at_** (something or someone)
    Examples:

- The people on the sidewalk *laughed at* the funny car driving down the street.
- All the students *laughed at* him because he said something funny.

To *listen to / for* (someone or something)
Example:
- We *listened to* the rap music.
- We walked along the street late at night in the dark and we *listened for* any unusual noise.
(Meaning: we *listened for* something means that we were trying to hear something)

To *look at / for* (something or someone)
Examples:
- We *looked at* the ocean for a hour.
- We were *looking for* the little girl. She was lost in the big department store.

To *look forward to* (something)
Examples:
- We are *looking forward to* going to Hawaii next month.
- Janice and Hiro were *looking forward to* the hiking trip.

To be _**mad at**_ (someone)
   Examples:
   - My boss _**was mad at**_ me because I didn't finish my work on time.
   - The customer _**was mad at**_ the bartender for giving him the wrong drink.

To be _**made of**_ (something)
   Examples: The house _**was made of**_ wood.
   The jar _**was made of**_ glass.

To be _**made for**_ (someone)
   Examples:
   - The dress _**was made for**_ that lady.
   - These shoes _**were made**_ especially _**for**_ me.

To be _**married to**_ (someone)
   Examples:
   - Ted _**is married to**_ Alice.
   - Darlene _**is married to**_ Don.

To _**matter to**_ (someone)
   Examples:
   - The project seemed small, but it _**mattered to**_ the company. (means: the project was important

to the company even though it was a small project).

- Money doesn't *matter to* some people. (🔍 means: money is not important to some people).

To be ***the matter with*** (someone or something)
Examples:
- I don't know what ***is the matter with*** this car, it won't start up! (🔍 Means: The car has a problem and the motor won't start)
- My brother was sick, but the doctors didn't know what ***was the matter with*** him.

To ***multiply*** (this) ***by*** (that)
Examples:
- If you ***multiply*** 10 ***by*** 10 the answer will be 100.
- ***Multiply*** 2 ***by*** 27 and the answer is 54.

To ***add*** (this) ***to*** / ***and*** (that)
Examples:
- If you ***add*** 10 ***to*** 10 the solution will be 20.
- ***Add*** 5 ***and*** 45 and the answer is 50.

To ***subtract*** (this) ***from*** (that)
Example:

- *Subtract* 10 *from* 15 and the answer is 5.
- If you *subtract* 100 *from* 1000 you get 900.

To *divide* (this) *by* (that)
Example:

- *Divide* 10 *by* 2 and the answer is 5.
- When 20 is *divided by* 2 the answer is 10.

Let's practice and review:

Read and / or listen to the following story and fill in the blanks with the correct preposition. Answers can be found in this chapter (above).

1. *Subtract* 15 _____ 30 and the answer is 15.

2. If you *add* 20 _____ 30 the solution will be 50.

3. What *is the matter* _____ this pen? It doesn't write!

4. Kaori *is married* _____ Kazu.

5. His wife *was mad* _____ him because he didn't take the garbage outside.

6. The building *was made* _____ stone.
7. The wedding dress *was made* ____ Yukiko.

8. If you *multiply* 5 ___ 5 the answer will be 25.

9. *Divide* 100 ___ 50 and the answer is 2.

10. The children are *looking forward* ___ going to the park tomorrow.

11. The people at he circus *laughed* ___ the funny clown.

12. We sat in the audience and *listened* ___ the orchestra.

Chapter 6
*Prepositions following verbs beginning with **N, O, P,** and **Q***

Using prepositions in expressions with certain verbs - N, O, P, and Q

If you have the Focus On English audio book that accompanies this lesson (available from your school store), listen carefully to the pronunciation of these expressions in sentences.

To be ***nervous about*** (something)
Examples:
- The actress *was nervous about* going on stage.
- The students *were nervous about* the exam.

To be ***nice to*** (someone)
Examples:
- The owner of the store *was nice to* the children and gave them some candy bars.
- Chris *is* always *nice to* his cousins.

To be ***opposed to*** (something)
Examples:
- The people of that country *were opposed to* high taxes.
- The local people of the island *were opposed to* having visitors.

To *pay for* (something)
  Examples:
  - The clerk in the food store waited for the man to *pay for* the food.
  - Please *pay for* your groceries at the checkout counter.

To be *patient with* (something or someone)
  Examples:
  - The teacher *was patient with* the new student.
  - My sister didn't do well in school, but the teachers were patient with her.

To be *pleased with* / *about* (something or someone)
  Examples:
  - Tomoko *was pleased with* the new bracelet that she just bought.
  - She *was* also *pleased about* getting such a good price.

To *point at* (something or someone)
  Examples:
  - The little girl *pointed at* the bird in the sky.
  - It is not polite to *point at* someone.

To be *polite to* (someone)
  Examples:
  - Jim was very *polite to* the older woman.

- It is not *polite to* point at someone.

To be *prepared for* (something)
Examples:
- Students, please *be prepared for* the final exam next week.
- The people of the town *were prepared for* the big storm.

To *protect* (something / someone) from (something / someone)
Examples:
- The mother *protected* the child *from* the cold rain with an umbrella.
- The police *protect* us *from* crime.

To be *proud of* (someone or something)
Examples:
- Keoki was very *proud of* his daughter because she received good grades on her exams.
- We are *proud of* our soccer team.

To be *qualified for* (something)
Examples:
- Eric *was qualified for* his new computer job. He had 4 years of training in the computer field.

- Joel was not *qualified for* the job he was doing.

Let's practice and review:

Read and / or listen to the following story and fill in the blanks with the correct preposition. Answers can be found in this chapter (above).

1. Jerry was very *polite* _____ the monks.

2. The teacher *was patient* _____ the beginning English students.

3. We *paid* _____ the food and left the restaurant.

4. Allison *was pleased* _____ the clothes she bought at the mall.

5. The guide *pointed* _____ mountains in the east.

6. We *weren't prepared* _____ the big storm that came quickly.

7. The applicant *wasn't qualified* _____ the job he wanted.

8. My friend was very *proud* _____ his sister because she received good grades on her exams.

9. The business *was nervous* _____ making the investment.

10. The shop owner *was nice* _____ to everyone who shopped there.

11. The president of the company *is opposed* _____ hiring more employees.

Chapter 7
*Prepositions following verbs beginning with **R** and **S***

Using prepositions in expressions with certain verbs - R and S

If you have the Focus On English audio book that accompanies this lesson (available from www.FOEBooks.com), listen carefully to the pronunciation of these expressions in sentences.

To be **_ready for_** (someone or something)
   Examples:
   - The doctor **_was ready for_** the next patient. We **_are ready for_** the long hike up the mountain. We have out boots and hiking equipment.
   - When you are camping in the wild, you should be prepared for anything.

To be **_related to_** (someone or something)
   Examples:
   - Bob Moore *is* not **_related to_** Kathy Moore. They come from different families.
   - This bad weather *is* not **_related to_** the storm that we heard about.

To **_rely on_** (someone or something)
   Examples:

- The employee was never on time and could not do his job right. His boss could not *rely on* him (could not trust him) to do a good job.
- We *relied on* our tour guide to take us back to the hotel.

To be *responsible for* (someone / something)
   Examples:
   - Jim was the manager of his division in his company. He *was responsible for* his employees and their work.
   - Peter *is responsible for* bringing the potato chips to the party.

To be *sad about* (something)
   Examples:
   - The little girl *was sad about* loosing her dog.
   - Jennifer *was sad about* missing the bus.

To be *safe from* (something)
   Examples:
   - The family went into the storm shelter to *be safe from* the hurricane.
   - Janet uses an anti-virus program on her computer to *be safe from* viruses.

To be **_satisfied with_** (someone /something)
> **Examples:**
> - Tomoko just bought a new car. She _was_ very **_satisfied with_** the car. The car was just the right color and was easy to operate.
> - Julie _**was satisfied with**_ her grade on the exam.

To be **_scared of / by_** (someone / something)
> **Example:**
> - The people in the city _**were scared of**_ the monster.
> - The young children _**were scared by**_ the loud noise on the street.

To **_search for_** (someone / something)
> **Examples:**
> - Jane could not find her car keys. She **_searched for_** them in her bedroom, living room and bathroom, but she could not find them.
> - The police **_searched for_** the missing child.

To **_separate_** (someone / something) **_from_** (someone / something)
> **Examples:**
> - The woman bought some beautiful red flowers and green flowers. The florist put all of the flowers together in one bag. When the woman took the

flowers home she *separated* the green flowers *from* the red flowers.

- The contest judges *separate* the good performances *from* the bad performances.

To be *sick of* (someone / something)
Examples:
- The student *was sick of* doing homework.
- Jack *was sick of* eating the same thing for lunch every day.

To be *similar to* (someone / something)
Examples:
- Janet went to the clothing shop to buy a dress. The clerk showed her a dress that *was* very *similar to* a dress that she already owned.
- This sports car *is* very *similar to* that one.

To be *slow at* (something)
Examples:
- The student *was slow at* learning math.
- In the beginning, the visitors *were* a little *slow at* understanding our culture.

To be *surprised at / by* (someone / something)
Examples:

- Hiroko _was surprised at_ the store's high prices for food.
- Everyone _was surprised at_ how expensive the dress was.

To _be_ / _feel sorry for_ (someone / something) _about_ (something)
  Examples:
  - The family lost all of their possessions in the terrible storm. We _feel_ very _sorry for_ them.
  - The boy broke the window with his soccer ball. He _was_ very _sorry for_ doing this.
  - The thief _was very sorry about_ stealing the little girl's money.

To _speak to_ (someone) _about_ (something)
  Examples:
  - Nicole _spoke to_ Tom about the problem she was having at work.
  - Maya _spoke to_ her travel agent about her trip to Europe.

To _stare at_ (someone / something)
  Examples:
  - Never _stare at_ the sun.
  - The two lovers _stared at_ each other for a long time.

To be ***sure of*** (someone / something)

   Examples:

- The student *was sure of* his answer. He wrote the answer on the test paper.

- Sandra was a confident person; she *was sure of* herself.

Let's practice and review:

Read and / or listen to the following story and fill in the blanks with the correct preposition. Answers can be found in this chapter (above).

1. Christine Smith ***is related*** ___ Allen Brock. They are brother and sister. Smith is Christine's married name.

2. You should not ***rely*** ___ other people to help you.

3. Stephan ***was responsible*** _____ maintenance of the company's cars.

4. Julie ***was sad*** _____ having to leave Hawaii after her vacation.

5. I went to my doctor and got a flu vaccine to ***be safe*** _____ the flu virus.

6. Allan's job at the factory is to ***separate*** the large parts _____ the small parts.

7. Annja **_searched_** _____ for her car keys but could not find them.

8. The children at the zoo **_were scared_** _____ the lion.

9. Peter **_was satisfied_** _____ the car he just bought.

10. The operator **_was sick_** ____ hearing complaints from callers.

11. Jean **_was surprised_** _____ the number of people who came to her party.

12. People usually **_feel_** very **_sorry_** _____ people who lose family members.

13. The students **_were slow_** ____ learning the new lesson.

14. A girl came to the party wearing a dress that **_was_** very **_similar_** ____ the dress that Kyoko was wearing.

15. The team **_was sure_** ____ it's ability to win the soccer match.

16. Never _stare_ _____ a stranger. It's impolite.

Chapter 8
*Prepositions following verbs beginning with **T through Z***

Using prepositions in expressions with certain verbs - T through Z

If you have the Focus On English audio book that accompanies this lesson (available from your school store), listen carefully to the pronunciation of these expressions in sentences.

To ***take care of*** (someone / something)
    Examples:
- The mother ***took care of*** the child.
- The businessman ***took care of*** the details needed to complete the business transaction.

To ***talk to / with*** (someone) about (something)
    Examples:
- The boy's father ***talked to*** him about his poor grades in school.
- The new employee ***talked with*** some of her colleagues about her new job.

To ***tell*** (someone) ***about*** (someone / something)
    Examples: The police ***told*** everyone ***about*** the prisoner that escaped.
    Mary told Christine about the new family who moved into the neighborhood.

To be **_terrible at_** (something)
    Examples:
- Jack **_was terrible at_** math. He never got good grades on his math exams.
- When I was in high school, I **_was terrible at_** history.

To be **_terrified by_** / **_of_** (someone / something)
    Examples:
- The little girl **_was terrified of_** the dark. She would never go outside of the house after dark.
- Jan's mother **_was terrified by_** snakes.

To **_thank_** (someone) **_for_** (something)
    Example:
- The old lady **_thanked_** the boy **_for_** helping her to cross the street.

To be **_tired of_** (someone or something): similar to **_sick of_**
    Example:
- The little boy **_was tired of_** eating vegetables at dinner time.

To be **_tired from_** (something)
    Examples:
- The man **_was tired from_** working so hard.
- Andrew **_was tired from_** the workout.

To *travel to* (somewhere)
   Examples:
   - The girl and her boyfriend *traveled to* Las Vegas together.
   - We plan on *traveling to* Indonesia this summer.

To be *used to* (something)
   Examples:
   - Jim walks to school every day. Walking to school was not a problem for Jim because he *was used to* doing it. (Same meaning as accustomed to)
   - Megumi *is used to* spending many hours studying English.

To *wait for* (someone or something)
   Examples:
   - The people in the theater *waited for* the show to begin.
   - We *waited for* the train for one hour.

To *wait on* (someone)
   Examples:
   - The waiter in the restaurant *waited on* the customers.
   - The stewardess *waited on* the airline passengers.

To be **_worried about_** (someone or something)
   Examples:
   - The mother _was worried about_ her sick child.
   - Toby _was worried about_ his friend who was in the hospital.

Let's practice and review:

Read and / or listen to the following story and fill in the blanks with the correct preposition. Answers can be found in this chapter (above).

1. The nurse _waited_ ____ her seriously ill patients.

2. The principal of the school _was used_ ____ hearing the excuses of the late students.

3. We _traveled_ _____ Honolulu last year.

4. The hikers _were tired_ _____ walking so much.

5. The big, strong man _was terrified_ _____ spiders.

6. The manager _thanked_ his workers _____ their hard work.

7. The policeman _talked_ ____ Jenny _____ her expired drivers license.

8. Fred *was terrible* _____ English grammar.

9. The lady next door *told* everyone _____ Mika's new boyfriend.

10. The baby sitter *took care* _____ the two children.

11. Everyone at the bus stop *waited* _____ the 12:05 bus.

12. The students **were worried** _____ the exam.

Mastering English Prepositions

Section 3: understanding the meanings and correct usage of all common English prepositions

Learn to use English prepositions correctly in all kinds of English sentences and conversation.

In this section, the student will find a comprehensive listing of the most commonly used prepositions in the English language, along with clear explanations about how to use them in different types of English sentences and plenty of examples to reinforce understanding.

The quick reference design will help the student to quickly find answers about any of the commonly used prepositions that we find in English communication.

If the student has the accompanying Focus On English mp3 audio book that goes with this book (sold separately in their school store or at www.FOEBooks.com), then he or she will be able to listen to and practice the examples. This listening / reading / speaking approach to learning is a good way to help the student build his or her knowledge of the correct use of prepositions in English sentences while improving pronunciation and oral sentence pattern awareness.

Chapter 1
*English prepositions beginning with the letters **A** and **B***

This is a comprehensive listing of the most common English prepositions. The prepositions are followed by a usage explanation. After each explanation there are examples to help reinforce the correct use of the preposition in common English sentences. If you have the accompanying Focus On English mp3 audio book, each example will be spoken twice and you can practice and reinforce your knowledge by repeating the examples with the teacher.

Common English prepositions beginning with the letters A and B

Below we will discuss these commonly used prepositions and provide you with many examples. Listen carefully to the pronunciation and, if you can, repeat the examples along with the teacher.

About:

*Usually we use the word **about** before a topic or person:*
Examples:
- They are talking ***about*** the plan for next week.
- The newspaper story is ***about*** the bank robbery that took place last night.
- She is not talking ***about*** you she is talking about Betty.

Page 90

About can also mean preparing to or getting ready to do something:
> **Example:**
>> ❏ She was *about* to leave when suddenly it began to rain.

Sometimes we use the word about to help describe a noun:
> **Example:**
>> ❏ There is something scary about that dark house.

Other non-prepositional uses for the word about:
> **Examples:**
>> ❏ He did an *about*-face (meaning: he changed his direction by 180 degrees).
>> ❏ It's *about* time! You're late! We have been waiting for more than three hours.

Note: about is also an adverb. The adverb about means almost:
> **Example:**
>> ❏ They are *about* done with the exam.

Above: (the opposite of above is below)

Usually, above means higher than or over:
> **Examples**
>> ❏ Oh look at that bird flying *above* our heads.

Page 91

- Look, this is very easy to understand. The ceiling is *above* us and the floor is beneath us. Got it?
- There are no subways in this city; all the trains travel *above* ground. (Our city has a good subway system; the trains travel *below* ground.)

Sometimes above is used in a sentence to talk about a good person that has good values and judgment and would not do something wrong:
Example:
- The Buddhist monk is *above* stealing.

Sometimes above is used like in the above sentence but to mean that a person wrongly believes that they are better than, for example, the law.
Example:
- The politician thought that he was *above* the law. (meaning: the politician wrongly believed that he could commit crimes because he thought that he was higher than the law).

Sometimes when you are reading something and it says to see something above. This means to look for something that was written before the section you are now reading.
Example:
- If you are having trouble using your new mp3 player, please see the *above* instructions.

Across:

Across is usually used to talk about movement from one side to the other side of a space, area, or location:

Examples:
- The man walked *across* the street to visit his secret lover.
- The tiny boat sailed *across* the great Pacific Ocean.
- The satellite flew *across* the sky at great speed.

Across is often used to mean directly facing something or someone:

Example:
- The bank was directly *across* from the food store. (Meaning: the bank's location and the food store's location were across from or facing each other)

Other uses for the preposition across:

Example:
- I came *across* a big sale while I was at the shopping mall. (Meaning: I discovered something I didn't expect to find while I was shopping.) Please see the Focus on English book for Phrasal Verbs for more information.

After: (the opposite of after is before)

After is usually used to mean *following* or *later than:*
Examples:
- There was a big dinner *after* the wedding ceremony, and the bride and groom were toasted many times.
- Dessert came *after* the main course, and it was delicious.
- I will be ready to go *after* 9am; please don't rush me.
- *After* breakfast, we went to the zoo and saw the new baby elephant.

After is used to mean something that happens continuously:
Example:
- The student studied night *after* night for the final exam.

After is often used to mean to chase or to be in pursuit of:
Example:
- The soccer player ran *after* the ball.

After can be used as a conjunction to connect two parts of a sentence:
Example:
- The teacher congratulated me *after* I received a high mark.

Please see the Focus on English book about Gerunds and Infinitives for more information about gerunds that follow prepositions.

Against:

Against can mean something forcibly hitting into or touching something else:
   Example:
   - He hit the tennis ball *against* the wall, but he didn't hit it very hard.

Against is usually used to mean to lean on or touch something or someone for support:
   Example:
   - You are such a lazy husband. The ladder is *against* the wall in the garage. Use this ladder to help to paint the house.

Against can mean in opposition to something:
   Example:
   - The people of the town were *against* higher taxes.

Against can also mean something that may not be an advantage; a disadvantage:
   Example:
   - They tried to repair the railroad tracks as quickly as possible, but time was *against* them; the next train would soon arrive.

Other uses for the preposition against:

- *Against* all odds, Hiro won the tournament.

Ahead of:

Ahead of usually means to be located in front of:
>**Example:**
- Kazu was ahead of Katrina in the lunch line.
  (Meaning, Katrina was closer to where lunch was being served than Kazu was.)

Ahead can sometimes mean that someone or something is more advance than someone or something else:
>Example:
- The student registered for classes one week late and so the other students were *ahead of* him.

  Meaning: the other students had already been studying for one week. The new student was new to the class work.)

Along:

Along usually means following the boundary of something:
>**Example:**
- There were beautiful flowers (all) *along* the road.

Along can mean together:
>Example:

- My friend Don decided to drive to Dallas, Texas. I decided to go *along* for the ride.

*Please refer to the Focus on English book on Phrasal Verbs, for more information about the word **along**.*

Among:

Among usually means surrounded by, included in a group, or many things or people in a group:
   Examples:
   - See, over there. You can see the house *among* the trees. There are ghosts in that house.
   - The party was a lot of fun. I was *among* my friends so I felt very comfortable. We had a blast.

Around:

Around can mean: follow a route (sometimes almost circular) to a desired location; located on the farther side of:
   Example:
   - The shopping center is *around* the corner from the bank, and two stores down from Wal-Mart. It's close to the park.

Around can mean following a boundary in a circular direction:
   Examples:

- For exercise we walk *around* the park, and then we do yoga and tai chi.
- The man traveled *around* the world by foot.

Around can mean walking or moving in many different directions randomly:
Example:
- We walked *around* the car show for about an hour and then we went home. We saw many interesting concept cars there.

*Please refer to the Focus on English book about phrasal verbs, and Focus on English book about idioms and expressions for more information about the word **around**.*

As:

As can mean: in the role of:
Example:
- Marco works *as* a mail clerk for the postal service.

*Please refer to the Focus on English book about phrasal verbs, and the Focus on English book about idioms and expressions, for more information about the word **as**.*

At:

At is often used in expressing time:
   Example:
   - I have to be at the dentist office *at* 10 o'clock. Oh, I don't want to go!

At is often used in talking about location:
   Examples:
   - He sat *at* his desk and sent emails to his girl friends.
   - Example: There was someone *at* the door with a big package. I was so surprised.
   - Example: We have to be *at* the show at 9pm, otherwise they will not allow us to enter the theater.

At is used to express a level or rate:
   Examples:
   - The food store is selling tomatoes *at* $1.00 per pound. Boy, that's cheap!
   - She is a good student. She is *at* the top of her class.

At is sometimes used to express rate of speed:
   Example:
   - The policeman stopped him and told Martin that he was driving too fast. Martin was traveling *at* 75 miles per hour when the policeman saw him.

*There are many uses for the word *at* after certain English verbs, in English phrasal verbs, and in English expressions (or idioms). Please refer to Focus On English book on phrasal verbs, and our Focus On*

English book about English idioms and expressions (available from your school store or from FOEBooks.com.)

Before: (the opposite of before is after)

<u>Before</u> *is sometimes used in expressions of time, as in: earlier than a certain time:*
   Examples:
   - The new student arrived in class <u>*before*</u> 9am.
   - The bus usually arrives <u>*before*</u> 4pm.
   - Oh no, we have to be at school <u>*before*</u> 8am tomorrow morning because we have to prepare a presentation for the class. Oh, I can't get up that early!

<u>Before</u> *is sometimes used to express order:*
   Examples:
   - The B train comes <u>*before*</u> the J train. If you miss the B train you will have to wait for 1 hour for the next B train.
   - The letter A comes <u>*before*</u> the letter B in the English alphabet.

<u>Before</u> *is sometimes used to express the position of someone or something in relationship to something else:*
   Examples:
   - The student was asked to stand <u>*before*</u> the class and give her presentation.

- The politician stood *before* the crowd and gave a speech.

Behind: (the opposite of behind is ahead)

Behind is sometimes used to express on the other side of something or someone; or to the rear of something:
   Examples:
   - The mouse is *behind* the wall, and it sounds like he's playing a clarinet.
   - She hid her face *behind* her scarf because she was laughing at the boy who seemed so interested in her.

Behind is sometimes used in expressions of time, meaning late or not on schedule:
   Example:
   - We were supposed to finish the project yesterday, but we are *behind*.

Below: (the opposite of below is above)

Below is used to talk about rank, position or location in comparison to something or someone else:
   Examples:
   - We live in a valley *below* a big mountain. (location)
   - The dish soap is in the cabinet *below* the sink. (location)

- The assistant director is *below* (lower in rank) the director. (rank)

Beneath (similar in meaning to the preposition *underneath*):

Beneath means under something and sometimes hidden or concealed by something:
Examples:
- Your feet are *beneath* the desk. Do I need to tell you that?
- The rug is *beneath* your feet. Please take off your shoes because the rug is new.

Beneath can be used to mean that something or someone is less worthy than someone or something else:
Examples:
- I am well educated and have plenty of experience. That job is for people with no education or experience. That job is *beneath* me. I am better than that.
- How dare you accuse me of stealing! I come from a very good family with high virtues. Stealing is *beneath* me. (Meaning: I am too virtuous to commit a crime).

Beside (similar in meaning to *next to*):

Beside means very close by, next to:
   Examples:
   - My friend stood *beside* me while I applied for citizenship.
   - Your bicycle is *beside* the house.
   - The pencil is there, *beside* your book.

Beside can also be used to mean very upset, agitated or emotional:
   Examples:
   - The mother was *beside* herself when she heard that her daughter was in the hospital.
   - The man who won the lottery was *beside* himself with joy.

Besides means in addition to:
   Examples:
   - *Besides* being the best student in the school, she was also a good athlete. (meaning: in addition to)
   - You are not old enough to drink alcohol, and *besides* that, alcohol is not good for you. (meaning: in addition to)

Between:

Between is used to talk about location of something, usually in the middle of two other things or people:
- **Examples:**
  - ❑ The grocery store is located *between* the bank and the library.
  - ❑ I found my homework. It was *between* the first and second page of my grammar book.

Between is sometimes used in expressions of time: from (beginning with) one time to (ending with) another time:
- **Examples:**
  - ❑ We eat lunch *between* 12pm and 1pm every day.
  - ❑ School is closed *between* June 1st, and August 1st.

Between is sometimes used to express sharing:
- **Examples:**
  - ❑ We went on our vacation with about $500 *between* us. (Meaning: together we had $500).
  - ❑ The ice cream cone costs $1.75, but we only had $1.50 *between* us. (Meaning: together we only had $1.50, 75 cents each, not enough for the ice cream cone)

There are other uses for the word *between* in English phrasal verbs and in English expressions (or idioms). Please refer to the **Focus On English** book about phrasal verbs, and the **Focus On English** book about Idioms and Expressions (available at your school store or at www.FOEBooks.com).

Beyond:

Beyond is used to express that something's or someone's location is further or on the other side of something / someone else :
>   **Examples:**
>   - Hello, I'm looking for the bank. Is it much further ahead?
>   No, only a kilometer *beyond* the gas station.
>   - Excuse me, where is the restroom?
>   The restroom is located just *beyond* the water fountain in that direction.

Beyond is sometimes used to express lack of understanding:
>   **Examples:**
>   - That math example was so hard. It was *beyond* me.
>   (Meaning: the math example was beyond my understanding, or my ability to understand it).
>   - I heard that Keiko got a passing grade on the exam. How she ever passed that exam without studying is *beyond* me!

Beyond can also be used to express being ahead of something or someone:
>   **Example:**

- She is a very good English student; she is _beyond_ me in grammar and writing. (Meaning: she is better than me at English grammar and writing)

By:

_By_ can be used in expression of time with the meaning **not later than**:
Examples:
- Why are you so worried? The teachers said that we have to have the homework done _by_ Wednesday at 8am!
- Hurry, we have to be there _by_ 5pm or we will miss the show.

_By_ can be used to talk about a **way** or **method** of doing something:
Examples:
- You can calculate the solution to that problem _by_ adding 5 and 8 together.
- I have to go to school _by_ bus tomorrow because my car broke down.
- I went to Fiji _by_ boat. Boy, that was a long trip.

_By_ can be used to can be used to mean **near** or **next to**:
Examples:
- My dog was sitting _by_ my side.

- He parked his car *by* my car. (Meaning: he parked his car next to my car.)

By can be used to express who or what caused something (usually used in passive sentences):
Examples:
- This house was built *by* a carpenter.
- The building was destroyed *by* the typhoon.
- The fingerprint marks on the wall were made *by* the child.

By can be used when talking about math; multiplication, division and expressing the measurements of rooms and geometric shapes:
Examples:
- The teacher told us that when we multiply 5 *by* 6 the answer is 30.
- All four pieces of candy cost $1.00. To calculate how much each piece of candy costs, divide $1.00 *by* 4. Each piece of candy costs 25 cents!
- The room measures 10 feet *by* 50 feet. That's a big room!

*There are other uses for the word *by* in English phrasal verbs and in English expressions (or idioms). Please refer to the Focus On English book about phrasal verbs and the Focus on English book about idioms and expressions (available in your school store or at www.FOEBooks.com).*

Chapter 1 <u>review</u>

*Prepositions beginning with the letters **A** and **B***
*Instructions: read and / or listen carefully to the sentences below. Decide whether the use of the preposition is correct or incorrect. If incorrect, which of these prepositions **best** fits the sentence:*
<u>about</u>, <u>above</u>, <u>across</u>, <u>after</u>, <u>against</u>, <u>ahead o</u>f, <u>along</u>, <u>among</u>, <u>around</u>, <u>as</u>, <u>at</u>, <u>before</u>, <u>behind</u>, <u>below</u>, <u>beneath</u>, <u>beside</u>, <u>besides</u>, <u>between</u>, <u>beyond</u>, <u>by</u>. *The answers can be found in this chapter (above).*

1. Alfred is talking <u>about</u> the exam he took last night.
   ☐correct ☐incorrect

2. The military planes are flying <u>beneath</u> our heads.
   ☐correct ☐incorrect

3. The grocery store was directly <u>by</u> the street from the library. ☐correct ☐incorrect

4. The policeman ran <u>among</u> the criminal. ☐correct ☐incorrect

5. The new bicycle is <u>against</u> the wall in the garage.
   ☐correct ☐incorrect

6. Lila was <u>ahead</u> of Alicia and Tommy in the registration line. ☐correct ☐incorrect

7. There were many people <u>among</u> the road during the marathon. ☐correct ☐incorrect

8. Many people walk <u>around</u> the mall for exercise.
☐correct ☐incorrect

9. William works as a pizza maker for the pizza shop <u>on</u> the corner. ☐correct ☐incorrect

10. Mika sat <u>between</u> the table and read a book. ☐correct ☐incorrect

11. You are not late for work if you arrive <u>before</u> 9am.
☐correct ☐incorrect

12. The vice president is <u>about</u> the president in rank.
☐correct ☐incorrect

13. The new floor tile is <u>beneath</u> my feet. ☐correct ☐incorrect

14. Your bicycle is <u>above</u> the house. ☐correct ☐incorrect

15. You can find the bank <u>between</u> the pet store and the fire station. ☐correct ☐incorrect

16. The grocery store is located just <u>along</u> the water fountain. ☐correct ☐incorrect

Chapter 2
*English prepositions beginning with the letters **C** - **F***

This is a comprehensive listing of the most common English prepositions beginning with the letters C through F. The prepositions are followed by a usage explanation. After each explanation there are examples to help reinforce the correct use of the preposition in common English sentences. If you are using the Focus on English audio book for this topic, each example will be spoken twice. You can practice and reinforce your knowledge by repeating the examples with the teacher on this mp3.

Common English prepositions beginning with the letters C - F

Below we will discuss these commonly used prepositions and provide you with many examples. If you have the mp3 audio book that accompanies this book, listen carefully to the pronunciation and repeat the examples along with the teacher.

Close to:

Close to is used to express nearness or nearly (almost):
    Examples:
- Where is the shopping mall?
  The shopping mall is ***close to*** the park.

- I am very *close to* my family.
- I received *close to* 100 emails this morning (meaning, almost 100 emails)! I'm tired of spam!

Despite:

Despite (In Spite Of) is used with a similar meaning to **even though** *or* **notwithstanding**:

Examples:
- *Despite* the rain, we will still have a picnic.
- He did well on the exam *despite* the difficult questions.
- He can kick a soccer ball hard *despite* the fact that he has weak legs.

Down:

Down is used with a similar meaning to **along** *when talking about travel:*

Examples:
- We walked *down* the road for about 2 miles and then stopped at the lake.
- My friend drove *down* the highway at about 100 miles per hour. I was really scared!

Down is used to talk about going from a higher place to a lower place:

Examples:
- The divers went *down* to the bottom of the lake.
- He was playing cards with his friends and he was loosing money. He threw the cards *down* on the table in anger.

There are other uses for the word down in English phrasal verbs and in English expressions (or idioms). Please refer to the Focus On English book on phrasal verbs, and the Focus On English book on idioms and expressions.

During:

During is used in expressions of time; meaning **within a period of time** *or meaning* **at the same time as something else is happening:**

Examples:
- I wrote my friend an email *during* the morning break. (within a period of time)
- I got up *during* the show and bought my girlfriend some popcorn. (at the same time as the show was occurring)

Far From:

Far From is used to talk about distance with the meaning that something is located far from something else:
>   **Examples:**
>   - The airport was *far from* the city center.
>   - Everyone moved *far* away *from* the entrance so that other people could enter the room easily.

For:

Use <u>For</u> in conversation to indicate a special purpose for something or someone:
>   **Examples:**
>   - He uses a motorcycle *for* transportation.
>   - She wears that outfit *for* the beach.
>   - Do you give a gift to your girlfriend when she gets a good grade on her exams? No, I usually don't give gifts *for* that reason.
>   - My friend gave me a gift *for* Christmas.
>   - We wore costumes *for* Halloween.

Use <u>For</u> in conversation to talk about time (usually length of time or to indicate future time):
>   **Examples:**
>   - I have been in New York *for* 3 months. (length of time)
>   - I have been studying English *for* 2 years. (length of time)

- I am studying now *for* the test next week. (future time)

Use *For* to express who or what is the recipient:
Examples:
- The played the song *for* him.
- My wife has a gift *for* me.
- The engineer has some information *for* his boss.
- I bought gas *for* the car.

Use *For* to explain the reason or benefit of doing something:
Examples:
- The student apologized *for* getting a bad grade. (reason)
- The woman was paid *for* cleaning the house. (reason)
- The boy was scolded *for* stealing the apple. (reason)
- We go surfing *for* fun. (benefit)
- We speak English to everyone *for* practice. (benefit)

Use *For* to talk about financial transactions:
Examples:
- Apples are $5 *for* 3 pounds.
- After he repaired the woman's car, he handed her a bill *for* $1,000!
- How much does he get paid?
  He works *for* $10 an hour.

Use *For* to express an unusual talent or sense:

Examples:
- Marco can sing any song just by listening to it! He has an ear *for* music.
- That woman has an eye for good art. She buys and sells art *for* an art gallery.

Use For to express an unusual fact:
Examples:
- That woman has big feet *for* such a small person.
- Boy, it's really cold *for* July!

There are other uses for the word *for* in English phrasal verbs and in English expressions (or idioms). Please refer to the Focus On English book about phrasal verbs and the Focus on English book on idioms and expressions for more information.

From: (the opposite of from is to)

From can be used in expressions of time:
Examples:
- The advanced English course runs *from* April 1st through April 30th. (*From*, in this example, has the meaning of 'beginning on.')
- The celebration runs *from* 5pm on. (*From* 5pm until an unknown time in the future)
- We will see the exhibit one month *from* today.
  (Meaning: one month's time, beginning today)

From can be used to indicate where something came from, source:
> **Examples:**
> - I got a letter *from* my friend in China.
> - Peaches come *from* Georgia.
> - The brother and sister get money *from* their parents.
> - He doesn't come *from* Europe. He comes *from* South Africa.

From can be used to indicate source + separation:
> **Examples:**
> - She borrowed money *from* her friend. (The friend was the source and money was separated *from* her and was lent to her friend).
> - The scientists tried to protect the whales *from* harm. (Separating the whales from harm)

From can be used to indicate distance (+ separation) away:
> **Examples:**
> - My aunt lives 25 miles *from* here.
> - New York City is 2,905 miles *from* San Francisco.
> - The racing cars raced passed us and then disappeared *from* view very quickly.

From is used in discussing math, especially subtraction:
> **Examples:**
> - Two *from* four equals two.
> - 100 *from* 1000 = 900

From can answer the question **why**:
Examples:
- They are tired *from* running all day.
- They are overweight *from* eating too much.

From can be used to talk about what something is made of:
Examples:
- The sweater was made *from* wool.
- The shoes were made *from* leather.
- The apple tree was grown *from* a seed.

From can be used to talk position in relation to something or someone else (usually referring to viewing or listening):
Examples:
- We can see the fireworks *from* our window.
- I could hear the speech *from* the back of the room.

There are other uses for the word from in English phrasal verbs and in English expressions (or idioms). Please refer to the Focus On English book about phrasal verbs and also about idioms and expressions for more information (available at your school store or at www.FOEBooks.com).

Chapter 2 <u>review</u>

Prepositions beginning with the letters **C** *through* **F**
Instructions: read and / or listen carefully to the sentences below. Decide whether the use of the preposition is correct or incorrect. If incorrect, which of these prepositions **best** *fits the sentence:* **<u>close</u>**

to, despite, down, during, far from, for, from. The answers can be found in this chapter (above).

1. Go <u>down</u> the road for about 3 miles, and then turn left at the red light. ☐correct   ☐incorrect

2. A student raised his hand <u>close to</u> the class and asked a question. ☐correct   ☐incorrect

3. The library is <u>far from</u> the school building. ☐correct   ☐incorrect

4. The workers use the machine <u>except</u> digging the earth. ☐correct   ☐incorrect

5. Jean received an email <u>close to</u> her friend in Spain. ☐correct   ☐incorrect

6. The members of the soccer team are tired <u>from</u> the workout. ☐correct   ☐incorrect

7. <u>Despite</u> the bad weather, our team won the match. ☐correct   ☐incorrect

8. I went for a swim <u>during</u> the afternoon. ☐correct   ☐incorrect

9. Alex borrowed money <u>down</u> Tricia. ☐correct ☐incorrect

10. The company sells products <u>for</u> a profit. ☐correct ☐incorrect

Chapter 3
*English prepositions beginning with the letters **I** - **N***

This is a comprehensive listing of the most common English prepositions beginning with the letters *I* - *N*. The prepositions are followed by a usage explanation. After each explanation there are examples to help reinforce the correct use of the preposition in common English sentences. If you for the Focus on English mp3 audio book for this topic each example will be spoken twice by the teacher. You can practice and reinforce your knowledge by repeating the examples with the teacher on this mp3.

Common English prepositions beginning with the letters I - N

Below we will discuss these commonly used prepositions and provide you with many examples. Again, if you have the mp3, listen carefully to the pronunciation and repeat the examples along with the teacher.

In:

In is used to talk about a person's or thing's location inside of something:
>**Examples:**
> - She was sitting *in* the room.
> - He was watching television *in* his house.
> - The pen was *in* the drawer.

In is used to talk about a location direction:
>   **Examples:**
> - The sun sets *in* the west.
> - Beautiful woven rugs are made *in* the east.

In is used to talk about being inside of a location boundary, city, country, state, etc:
>   **Examples:**
> - Right now, we are *in* New York City.
> - My friend lives *in* San Francisco.
> - Tokyo is *in* Japan.
> - We are *in* the park.

(What is the difference between *at* the park and *in* the park? We say that we are *in* the park when we are within the boundaries of the park. We often say we are *at* the park when we have arrived near to the park boundary. Sometimes, English speakers use *in* and *at* interchangeably when referring to locations like airport, library, school, park, etc. Example: Where are you now? I'm *at* the park; or, I'm *in* the park. Generally, *at* refers to being located close to or on the border of a location, whereas *in* refers to being inside the boundaries of the location.)

In is used to talk about time:
>   **Examples:**
> - He was born in Okinawa, *in* 1983.

- I'm late! I have to be at school *in* 10 minutes!
- My wife should be home *in* 2 hours.
- We usually start school *in* September.
- My mother will be arriving *in* two weeks.
- They take their shower *in* the morning.
- We watch the sun set *in* the evening.
- I think we were happier *in* the 1970s. (or: *in* the 70s)

Use *In* when talking about weather:
Examples:
- We like to walk *in* the rain.
- It's hot *in* the sun.

Use *In* when talking about what someone is wearing:
Examples:
- She went to dinner *in* a beautiful black dress.
- They went to the Halloween party *in* a funny costume.

Use *In* when talking about a location on the body:
Examples:
- He was hit *in* the chest.
- She put her contact lens *in* her eye.
- The soccer player has a pain *in* his foot.

Use *In* when talking how people relate to each other:
Examples:
- They were *in* an argument last night.

- All of the members of the group worked *in* cooperation with each other to solve the problem.
- The mother asked the little boy why his shirt was torn.
    The little boy told his mother that he was *in* a fight.

Use In when talking about the current status of something or someone:
Examples:
- The old book is still very popular. It is still *in* print.
- That recipe is very famous and is *in* demand. Meaning: many people would like to have it)

Use In when you want to be clear about measurement:
Examples:
- He is very heavy. I don't know what he weighs *in* kilos, but *in* pounds he weighs more than 300.
- The car is very tall *in* height.

There are many other uses for the word *in* in English phrasal verbs and in English expressions (or idioms). Please refer to the Focus On English books on phrasal verbs and idioms and expressions (available at your school store or at www.FOEBooks.com).

In Back of:

In Back of means to the rear of *or* behind:

Examples:
- They keep the garbage cans *in back of* the building.
- The garage is *in back of* the house.

In Front of:

In Front of refers to something or someone that is located before or facing something or someone:

Examples:
- The woman stood *in front of* the mirror combing her hair.
- The car was parked *in front of* the school building.

Inside:

Inside refers to something or someone that is located within something else:

Examples:
- The pencils are *inside* that red box.
- The two girls are *inside* that house.

Instead of:

Instead of means to substitute something for something else:

Examples:
- We went swimming *instead of* surfing.
- Kazu studied English *instead of* Italian.

Into:

Into is used to mean **enter:**
Examples:
- The businessman stepped *into* the cab.
- The English student went *into* the classroom.
- The flower shop girl put the flowers *into* a bag.

Into is sometimes used to mean **something of interest** *or an* **occupation** *or* **preoccupation:**
Examples:
- The students are really *into* learning English. (The students really enjoy learning English.)
- He loves soccer; he is really *into* soccer!

Into is sometimes used to talk about math division:
Examples:
- 12 *into* 48 equals 4.
- Ten *into* one hundred equals ten.

Into is used to talk about a condition change:
Examples:
- The student got *into* trouble for cheating on the exam.
- Kyoko got *into* debt after buying the expensive home.

Into is used to talk about sudden, hard contact, or forced contact with something or someone:
> Examples:
> - The motorcycle crashed *into* the building but the driver was not seriously hurt.
> - The girl ran *into* the tree and had to be taken to the hospital.

*There are many other uses for the word **into** in English phrasal verbs and in English expressions (or idioms). Please refer to Focus On English books about phrasal verbs and English expressions and idioms (available at your school store or at www.FOEBooks.com.)*

Like:

Like is used to talk about similarities:
> **Examples:**
> - There is no other person *like* him.
> - Places *like* New York and Los Angeles can be interesting vacation stops.
> - He is *like* his brother. They both enjoy playing sports.

*Like is used to talk about **examples**:*
> **Examples:**
> - There are many forms of transportation, *like* cars, trains and planes.

- There are many things you can do to improve your English, *like* talking to native speakers, studying grammar, and attending classes regularly.

Near:

Near is used to talk about distance from or location; something that is **close by:**
- **Examples:**
  - Oh, look at the tall buildings, we must be *near* Dallas.
  - The whiteboard is *near* the door.

Next to:

Next to is used to talk about something or someone that is near, close to, or in very close proximity to:
- **Examples:**
  - She parked her car *next to* mine in the mall parking lot.
  - Could you tell me where the grocery store is? Yes, it is *next to* the bank on Smith Street.

Chapter 3 review

Prepositions beginning with the letters **I - N**
Instructions: read and / or listen carefully to the sentences below. Decide whether the use of the preposition is correct or incorrect. If

incorrect, which of these prepositions **best** fits the sentence: *in*, *in back of*, *in front of*, *inside*, *instead of*, *into*, *like*, *near*, *next*. The answers can be found in this chapter (above).

1. I waited <u>in near of</u> the taxi stand for two hours, but no taxi came. ☐correct ☐incorrect

2. The car is <u>inside</u> the garage. ☐correct ☐incorrect

3. The businessman went <u>into</u> the building. ☐correct ☐incorrect

4. Places <u>like</u> Honolulu and Cancun can be nice places to vacation. ☐correct ☐incorrect

5. Long Island is <u>instead of</u> New York City. ☐correct ☐incorrect

6. The bus stopped <u>next to</u> the shopping center. ☐correct ☐incorrect

7. One hundred <u>near</u> one thousand equals ten. ☐correct ☐incorrect

8. We went swimming <u>instead of</u> surfing. ☐correct ☐incorrect

9. Jim and Nancy got <u>into</u> debt when they bought the expensive sports car. ☐correct ☐incorrect

10. The restrooms are <u>in</u> <u>back</u> <u>of</u> the plane . ☐correct ☐incorrect

Chapter 4
English prepositions beginning with the letter O

This is a comprehensive listing of the most common English prepositions beginning with the letter _O_. The prepositions are followed by a usage explanation. After each explanation there are examples to help reinforce the correct use of the preposition in common English sentences. If you have the mp3 audio book version of this book, you will notice that each example is spoken twice. You can practice and reinforce your knowledge by repeating the examples with the teacher on this mp3.

Common English prepositions beginning with the letter O

Below we will discuss these commonly used prepositions and provide you with many examples.

Of:

Of is used to talk about **belonging to** *or* **being connected to** *a group, something, someone or time:*
>   **Examples:**
> - Who is that tall man there?
>   He is the dean _of_ this college.
> - That monk is _of_ the Buddhist religion.
> - That man is a citizen _of_ the USA.
> - Who is she?
>   She is a doctor _of_ medicine.

- The author is writing a book on the trees and plants *of* Australia.
- We watched fireworks on the fourth *of* July.
- April Fools day is on the first day *of* April.
- I finished my English studies in March *of* last year.

Of *is used to help talk about* **categories** *or* **types** *of things or people:*

Examples:
- He was very embarrassed; the color *of* his face was red.
- The cost *of* the home was very high.
- Before you can order shoes, you have to know the size *of* your foot.
- I don't like the smell *of* that fish. I think it is bad.
- My mother bought two bags *of* rice yesterday.

Of *is used to help talk about quantity:*

Examples:
- Are we going to be late?
  No, we have plenty *of* time.
- Many *of* the people who listen to EnglishMP3 audio books learn English well.
- We have hundreds *of* products in our store.
- Don't worry about breaking the dish; we have plenty *of* dishes.

💡 *There are many other uses for the word **of** in English phrasal verbs and in English expressions (or idioms). Please refer to the Focus on English about phrasal verbs and the Focus on English about idioms and expressions (available from your book store or from www.FOEBooks.com.)*

Off:

***Off** is used to talk about a condition or state of being; that something is not on or has stopped functioning:*

Examples:
- The stove is cool. It must be *off*.
- Would you please turn *off* all the lights? Electricity is expensive.
- Well, that show was terrible. I think I will turn *off* the TV now.
- Did we turn the stove *off* before we left home?
  Yes, remember? I turned it *off* 10 minutes before we left the house.

***Off** is used to talk about **movement** that represents change in location:*

Examples:
- The papers blew *off* the table.
- The motorcycle ran *off* the road but the driver was not hurt.

Off can be used to mean **to remove** *or* **separate***:*
> **Examples:**
> - Mary, did you take your books *off* the counter? Yes mom, my books are *off* the counter.
> - My father shaved *off* his beard. Boy, his appearance really changed!

Off can be used to mean **to stop doing something***:*
> **Examples:**
> - Do you want to go to the club with me?
>   I can't because I'm *off* alcohol. (Meaning: I don't want to drink alcohol any more.)
> - What time do you get *off* work? (Meaning: What time do you stop work.)
>   I get *off* at 4pm.

Off is used to mean **not far from***:*
> **Examples:**
> - The bank is just *off* Elm Street. (Meaning: A little bit further past or in the vicinity of Elm Street.)
> - Oh, that was a terrible golf shot. You're a little *off* today. (Meaning: You are not playing like you usually do; your golf game is not as good as usual.)

Off is sometimes used in commands and warning signs to mean **do not have contact with***:*
> **Examples:**

- Please keep _off_ the grass!
- Wet concrete, keep _off_!

There are many other uses for the word _off_ in English phrasal verbs and in English expressions (or idioms). Please refer to the Focus On English books about phrasal verbs and about idioms and expressions (available from your school store or from www.FOEBooks.com.)

On:

_On_ can mean contact with a surface or surface location:
Examples:
- The books are _on_ the desk.
- The picture is _on_ the wall.
- The fly is _on_ the window.
- The writing is on the wall.
- The woman is driving her car _on_ the street.
- The boy is riding his skateboard _on_ the sidewalk.

_On_ can mean in contact but above something else:
Examples:
- Please print your name _on_ the line.

_On_ can mean a location, usually outdoors:
Examples:
- The parking garage is _on_ the side of the building.

- Where are you?
  We're _on_ the corner of Elm and Second Avenue.
- We went _on_ the roof to get the cat.
- We all live _on_ the planet called Earth.

_On_ is used to talk about time:
  Examples:
- I have to go to the doctor's office _on_ Wednesday.
- My family is coming to visit _on_ Christmas day.
- We will arrive _on_ Monday.

_On_ is used when talking about transportation and traveling:
  Examples:
- They got _on_ the bus.
- She was _on_ the train for two hours.
- The family spent four hours _on_ the plane.
- (Note: use _in_ when talking about a taxi or car.
  Example: The businessman was _in_ the taxi for an hour because of heavy traffic.)

_On_ is used to talk about membership or being part of something:
  Examples:
- My name is _on_ the good student list.
- He is _on_ the soccer team.

_On_ is used to talk about means or resource:

Examples:
- The space shuttle rocket runs _on_ special fuel.
- My wife and I live _on_ my paycheck.
- The three mountain climbers survived _on_ little water.

_On_ can sometimes indicate the cause of a mishap or problem:
Examples:
- The boy hurt himself _on_ his skateboard.
- She got sick _on_ the bad food she ate at the restaurant.

_On_ can sometimes indicate a reason for doing something:
Examples:
- They went to Fiji _on_ vacation.
- Michael went to New York _on_ business.

_On_ is sometimes used to indicate subject or topic; meaning about:
Examples:
- I read an article _on_ how to learn English quickly.
- Their class presentation was _on_ the environment.

_On_ can be used to indicate possession:
Examples:
- Can I borrow $5?
  Sorry, I don't have any money _on_ me.
- Excuse me. Do you have a pen _on_ you? I need to write down a phone number.

On is used to indicate a special occasion:
Examples:
- Congratulations *on* getting married.
- They celebrated by going out dancing *on* their anniversary.

On can indicate status, condition, or state:
Examples:
- Your new shoes are *on* order and should arrive next week.
- The woman is *on* a diet. She is trying to lose 30 pounds.

On can be used to indicate a **continuation** *of what was being done:*
Examples:
- After stopping at the motel, we drove *on* to our next destination.
- We stopped to look at the accident, but the police told us to move *on*.

On is used to talk about how something was communicated:
Examples:
- I learned about the new job opportunity *on* the Internet.
- I saw the advertisement *on* TV.
- Stefan and his brother heard the news *on* the radio.

On is used to talk about behavior towards something or someone:

Examples:
- The long days without food or water were hard *on* the survivors. It was the biggest challenge of their lives.
- The test was too easy *on* the students. Everyone got a very high mark!

On can help to express **adding** *to something or* **acquiring** *something:*

Examples:
- Jim wants to add *on* a bedroom to his house.
- The school added *on* five new teachers.

On can be used to express two things happening at the same time (in this usage, on and upon can be used simultaneously):

Examples:
- *On* second thought, he decided not to buy the car.
- He called the fire department *on* seeing the fire in the house.

On can be used to help express feelings or attitude towards something or someone:

Examples:

- The girl in the second row has a crush _on_ the boy in the front of the class. (Meaning: she has a romantic interest in him.)
- The man took pity _on_ the homeless man and gave him some money.

There are many other uses for the word _on_ in English phrasal verbs and in English expressions (or idioms). Please refer to the Focus On English books about phrasal verbs and expressions and idioms (available from your school store or from www.FOEBooks.com.)

Onto:

Onto *is used to talk about moving from one place to another place:*
Examples:
- The spider jumped _onto_ the table.
- It was raining so they moved all of the picnic food _onto_ a table that was under an umbrella.

Opposite:

Opposite *is used to mean across from:*
Examples:
- Excuse me. Could you tell me where the bank is located?

Yes. The bank is up that street *opposite* the grocery store.
- She sat *opposite* her boyfriend at the fancy restaurant.

Out:

Out is used when talking about passing something around or distributing something:
Examples:
- Sally, would you please pass *out* these forms to the class.
- We mailed *out* about 1,000 brochures to advertise our new business.

Out is used when talking about removing something or someone:
Examples:
- I brought the gift *out* to the car. I'm bringing it to my sister's birthday party.
- She opened the box and took *out* the new dress.

Out is often used with the preposition *of* in expressing different ideas in English. Below are some usage explanations and examples for *out of*.

Out of can be used to express absence:
Examples:

- Three *out* of five people today do not exercise regularly.
- Two *out* of every three of these apples are bad. We should take this bag of apples back to the market.

Out of can be used to express a percentage or fraction of something:
>   **Examples:**
> - Hello Marta. I haven't seen your sister in a week. Where is she?
>   Oh, she is *out of* the country. She will be back next week.
> - Mr. Yoshida is *out of* the office at the moment, may I take a message for him?
> - Hello? No, Gerhard is not here right now. He is *out of* town.

Out of can be used to express **not being normal** *or* **not what is usually expected***:*
>   **Examples:**
> - Oh my gosh, that coat is so *out of* style!
> - What happened?
>   That car went *out of* control and hit the telephone pole!

Out of can be used to express what something was made of or what ingredients went into making something:
>   **Examples:**

- That company makes surfboards *out of* bamboo.
- Cotton candy is made *out of* pure sugar.

Out of can be used to express a lack of or no longer available or in supply:
Examples:
- I drove to the gas station to get some fuel for my car, but the gas station was *out of* fuel.
- I would like to have a vanilla ice cream cone, please.

  Sorry. We are all *out of* vanilla. (Note: the word *all* used with *out of* means *completely*.)

Out of can mean **away from,** *similar to* **distance from:**
Examples:
- Excuse me. Could you tell me where the nearest gas station is?

  Yes. It's on this road about four miles *out of* town.
- If you want to buy alcohol, you will have to go *out of* state because it is illegal in this state to sell alcohol.

Out of can be used to express a reason for doing something:
Examples:
- I went to Bali *out of* curiosity. I've always wanted to see what that island was like.
- I adopted the stray cat *out of* pity.

There are many other uses for the word *out* in English phrasal verbs and in English expressions (or idioms). Please refer to the Focus on

English phrasal verbs book and the Focus on English idioms and expressions book for more information (available at your school store or at www.FOEBooks.com.)

Outside:

Outside is often used with the preposition of. Outside means not within the confines of something:
    Examples:
- We could hear strange noises *outside* the house.
- The man put his wet boots *outside* the door.

Over:

Over means above something or someone; it usually indicates being higher than:
    Examples:
- We flew *over* New York on our way to Boston.
- The branch of the tree hung *over* the house.
- The price of that car is expensive. It's way *over* my head because I don't earn that much money.
- I don't understand Einstein. His theories are way *over* my head. (Meaning: I can't understand his theories because they are too complicated for me.)

Over is used to mean **to cover something or someone:**

Examples:
- The workers put a steel plate *over* the hole in the road.
- It was cold in the room so she put a sweater on *over* her blouse.

Over is used to express **above and then to the other side of** *something or someone:*
Examples:
- The runner jumped *over* the branch that was in the road.
- The football player kicked the ball *over* the wall.
- We had to climb *over* the fence to get into the park.
- Is it possible to jump *over* a rainbow?
- You should drive your car slowly *over* a speed bump.

Over is used to express **control** *over something or someone:*
Examples:
- The emperor rules *over* the people in his country.
- The general manager of the company is *over* all employees.

Over is used to express **location away from** *and* **on the other side of** *something or someone else:*
Examples:
- The market is *over* there.

- I work in a building that is just _over_ the bridge.

  (Note: the word *just* is used to mean *a small distance from*.)

Over can be used to indicate **topic** or **subject**:
Examples:
- We fought _over_ who should pay the check at the restaurant.
- They leader of the country worried _over_ the shortage of food.

Over (adverb) can mean finished:
Examples:
- The show is _over_.
- School is _over_.

There are many other uses for the word **_over_** in English phrasal verbs and in English expressions (or idioms). Please refer to the Focus On English phrasal verbs book and the Focus on English idioms and expressions book (available from your school store or from FOEBooks.com).

Chapter 4 review

Prepositions beginning with the letter **O**

Instructions: read and / or listen carefully to the sentences below. Decide whether the use of the preposition is correct or incorrect. If *incorrect, which of these prepositions **best** fits the sentence: <u>of</u>, <u>off</u>, <u>on</u>, <u>onto</u>, <u>on top of</u>, <u>opposite</u>, <u>out</u>, <u>outside</u>, <u>over</u>. The answers can be found in this chapter (above).*

1. The priest is <u>of</u> the Catholic faith. ☐correct ☐incorrect

2. The final semester ends in June <u>on top of</u> this year. ☐correct ☐incorrect

3. My friend shaved the hair <u>off</u> his head. ☐correct ☐incorrect

4. The butter is <u>on</u> the table. ☐correct ☐incorrect

5. She was <u>out</u> the train for two hours. ☐correct ☐incorrect

6. The dancer jumped <u>onto</u> the stage. ☐correct ☐incorrect

7. The two buildings are <u>opposite</u> each other. ☐correct ☐incorrect

8. The student passed <u>of</u> the exam. ☐correct ☐incorrect

9. Jonathan is <u>out of</u> the country. ☐correct ☐incorrect

10. The two girls fought <u>over</u> the good-looking boy.
    ☐correct   ☐incorrect

Chapter 5
English prepositions beginning with the letters P - T

This is a comprehensive listing of the most common English prepositions beginning with the letters *P* - *T*. The prepositions are followed by a usage explanation. After each explanation there are examples to help reinforce the correct use of the preposition in common English sentences. Each example will be spoken twice. You can practice and reinforce your knowledge by repeating the examples with the teacher on this mp3.

Common English prepositions beginning with the letters P - T

Below we will discuss these commonly used prepositions and provide you with many examples.

Past:

Past is used to mean beyond:
    Examples:
- Excuse me. How do I get to the theater. Just go up this street *past* the stop light and the theater is on your left.
- The director's office is just *past* classroom number 3 on the right side of the hall.

Past can mean to go by something or someone:

Examples:
- The girl walks *past* the pastry shop on her way to school every day.
- We drove *past* Lincoln Center in New York City.

Since:

Since means continuously or intermittently from a time in the past until the present:
Examples:
- I haven't been in Tokyo *since* last September.
- The school has been open *since* 1995.
- He hasn't said hello *since* we had that argument.

Through:

Through can be used to express passage, or movement, across or under a potential barrier or obstacle:
Examples:
- The five limousines passed *through* the open gate.
- I got a ticket for going *through* a red light.
- As we walked *through* the door, our whole family was there to greet us.
- We drove *through* the tunnel without our lights on. Boy, it was dark in there.

Through can be used to mean contiguous or sequential (Meaning: one thing occurring in exact order after the other) with a beginning and an ending:
> **Examples:**
> - The students were asked to read pages 24 *through* 31 for their homework.
> - My dad works Monday *through* Friday at the factory.
> - The sale will continue on *through* Tuesday of next week.

Through can be used to express passage or movement within a confining space or borders:
> **Examples:**
> - We passed *through* the long, dark hallway as we walked to the waiting room.
> - We walked *through* the park on our way home.

Through can relate to vision; being able to see something beyond the initial surface:
> **Examples:**
> - We looked *through* the window and saw the city below.
> - My car needs new paint. I can see the metal showing *through* the paint in some spots.

Through is used to express completing something that may require hard work to finish:

Examples:
- I want to travel a lot, but first I have to get *through* school.
- That was a bad storm. I didn't think we were going to get *through* it.
- She went *through* a bad experience, but now she feels better.

Through is used with the word **all** to have the same meaning as **throughout** (Meaning: in all parts, or during an entire event):
Examples:
- My girlfriend and I walked all *through* the park looking at the gardens and enjoying the sunshine.
- That cat was crying all *through* the night. I hardly got any sleep!

Through is used to express the reason for something:
Examples:
- The student achieved high grades *through* hard work and study.
- The woman was overcharged for her purchase *through* a computer error.

Through is used to express the means by which something happens:
Examples:
- We got the information *through* his website.

- I got the job *through* an employment agency.

Throughout:

Throughout is used to express that something is occurring everywhere, in all parts of:
   Examples:
- There are yoga centers *throughout* New York City.
- There are fire alarm boxes *throughout* the building.

Throughout is used to talk about something occurring during an entire period of time:
   Examples:
- He has been a very successful person *throughout* his life.
- We ask that students remain silent *throughout* the exam.
- We partied *throughout* the whole Christmas holiday.

To:

To is used to indicate a response or reaction to something or someone:
   Examples:
- I hope you will agree *to* my offer.

- The teacher hoped that the students paid attention *to* the lesson.
- Her reaction *to* that comment was negative.
- The old man was grateful *to* receive the help.

To is used to indicate a destination:
Examples:
- The plane *to* L.A. will arrive at 5am.
- She wants sail *to* the South Pacific.
- The letter was *to* her.
- The sisters go *to* school every day, five days a week.

To is used to talk about time:
Examples:
- We work from 9am *to* 5pm every day.
- They worked on the project from morning *to* night.

Here is another way to is used to talk about time:
- The time is now 15 minutes *to* 6. (a quarter to six)
- It's 20 minutes *to* noon.

To is used to help express who or what receives something; meaning, beneficiary of something:
Examples:
- His company awarded the prize *to* him for his hard work.
- The city dedicated the monument *to* the memory of its famous writer.

- The school gave a scholarship *to* the student because of her good work.

To is used to help express transferring and exchanging something from a person or a place:
Examples:
- The secretary brings the mail *to* the office every day.
- The student read his presentation *to* the class.
- The hair dresser recommended the hair conditioner *to* the woman.
- "Would you please give that *to* me," said Oliver Hardy to Stan Laurel. "Thank you."

To is used to help express what **effect** someone or something has on someone or something else:
Examples:
- Please stop having loud parties every night! You are a nuisance *to* the neighborhood. (And, besides, you never invite me.)
- The new park has been a pleasing experience *to* everyone.
- To my embarrassment, I sent the email *to* the wrong person.

To can be used to refer to one's self in a sentence:
Examples:
- *To* her disappointment, she didn't get a good grade on the final exam.

- The work was completed *to* their satisfaction.

To is used to help express repetition:
Examples:
- Our boat trip across the bay was really uncomfortable. The boat rolled side *to* side.
- The homeless man went from house *to* house asking for food.

To is used to help express attaching something to something, or attachment:
Examples:
- She stapled the picture *to* the form.
- The carpenter nailed the wood *to* the floor.

To is used to help express comparison:
Examples:
- The sun is very bright here, compared *to* where I live.
- Your essay is very similar *to* mine.

To is used to indicate action caused by sound:
Examples:
- The next morning they woke up *to* the sound of the ocean.
- She tapped her fingers *to* the sound of the music.

To is used to help express relationship of one thing to another:

Examples:
- I'd like to introduce you to the new assistant *to* the director.
- These are the keys *to* my car. Please don't crash it.
- The school building is close *to* the mall.
- This street runs parallel *to* that one.
- There are 3.8 liters *to* one gallon.

To is used to help express extremes:
Examples:
- She was so mad that she tore the contract *to* bits.
- I'm trying to study and the noise from the party next door is driving me *to* madness.

To is used to help indicate problems or solutions:
Examples:
- Our water reservoirs are almost dry. This is a threat *to* our survival.
- What is your solution *to* this problem?

To is used to help express ownership or connectedness:
Examples:
- That house belongs *to* me.
- This issue is important *to* me.
- He is married *to* that woman.

To is used to help express restrictedness:
Examples:

- The teenager was confined *to* her room for disobeying her mother.
- The prisoners were restricted *to* two meals a day.

Please refer to Focus On English, <u>Mastering English Gerunds and Infinitives</u>, *for more uses of the word* *to*. *There are also many other uses for the word* *to* *in English phrasal verbs and in English expressions (or idioms). Please refer to the Focus On English books on phrasal verbs and idioms and expressions (available from your school store or from www.FOEBooks.com).*

Toward(s):

<u>Toward(s)</u> *is used to help express the direction to a location or place:*

Examples:
- The tourists headed *toward* the beach.
- We sailed our boat *toward* the island.
- How do I find the iPod store?
  To find the iPod store, walk *towards* the bank for about 5 minutes, and then look to your left. It's the third store past the bank.
- The plane took off and headed *toward* Paris, France.
- See, over there. Look *towards* the intersection. You can see a man playing music on the street corner and dancing in his bare feet.

<u>Toward(s)</u> *is used to help express contribution or making a partial payment:*

Examples:
- The couple made a contribution of $1,000 **_towards_** the sick man's medical bills.
- The boy pays $50 every month **_towards_** his car payment.

Toward(s) *is used to help express nearness to a certain time:*
Examples:
- We always get excited about going skiing **_towards_** the middle of the winter.
- The math student was getting nervous **_towards_** the end of the exam because time was running out.

Toward(s) *is used to help express attitude:*
Examples:
- The parents are very loving **_towards_** their children.
- The students were very respectful **_towards_** their teacher.

Toward(s) *is used to help express movement in the direction of some kind of action:*
Examples:
- They are working **_towards_** an agreement.
- Peter is heading **_towards_** a decision to leave the company.

Chapter 5 <u>review</u>

*Prepositions beginning with the letters <u>**P** – **T**</u>*

*Instructions: read and /or listen carefully to the sentences below. Decide whether the use of the preposition is correct or incorrect. If incorrect, which of these prepositions **best** fits the sentence: **<u>past</u>**, **<u>since</u>**, **<u>through</u>**, **<u>throughout</u>**, **<u>to</u>**, **<u>towards</u>**. The answers can be found in this chapter (above).*

1. I haven't been in Tokyo <u>since</u> 1999. ☐correct ☐incorrect

2. The students passed <u>through</u> the museum and looked at the works of art. ☐correct ☐incorrect

3. There were many questions <u>throughout</u> the company meeting. ☐correct ☐incorrect

4. The student was grateful <u>to</u> receive tutoring from the teacher. ☐correct ☐incorrect

5. As soon as we got to Hawaii we headed <u>since</u> the beach. ⊚correct ⊚incorrect

6. Barbara is married <u>past</u> Alex Smith. ☐correct ☐incorrect

7. Our group sang songs <u>throughout</u> the train journey.
   ☐correct ☐incorrect

8. Every time I walk <u>past</u> the pastry shop I get hungry.
   ☐correct ☐incorrect

9. We attend school Monday ***through*** Friday every week. ☐correct ☐incorrect

10. The leader of the country has been kind <u>*to*</u> everyone.
    ☐correct ☐incorrect

Chapter 6

English prepositions beginning with the letters U - Z

This is a comprehensive listing of the most common English prepositions beginning with the letters U - Z. The prepositions are followed by a usage explanation. After each explanation there are examples to help reinforce the correct use of the preposition in common English sentences. If the student has a copy of the Focus on English mp3 audio book for this topic, each example will be spoken twice by the teacher. You can practice and reinforce your knowledge by repeating the examples with the teacher on this mp3 audio book (available at your school store or at www.FOEBooks.com.)

Common English prepositions beginning with the letters U - Z

Below we will discuss these commonly used prepositions and provide you with many examples.

Under:

Under is used to mean being in a lower position than something or someone else:
   Examples:
   - The pen is *under* the table.
   - The man is walking *under* the bridge.

- The submarine can travel *under* water.

Under is used to help express being under the supervision of or control of something or someone:
  Examples:
  - She has been very sick. Currently, she is *under* the supervision of a doctor.
  - We are working *under* a manager that does not give us very much freedom.
  - That country continues to suffer *under* bad leadership.

Under is used to express **less than**:
  Examples:
  - You can buy that car for *under* $20,000.
  - Sorry, we can't sell you beer because you are *under* age 21.

Under can mean the same as *underneath* meaning **hidden or covered by something** else:
  Examples:
  - The cats hid *under* the house. We couldn't find them for days.
  - She hid her purse *under* the bed.
  - Sand crabs are found *underneath* the sand at the beach.
  - He found his driver's license *underneath* a pile of papers on his desk.

Under can be used to express a situation, condition or state:
> **Examples:**
> - The website is *under* construction and should be done next month.
> - The man was sent to jail for causing trouble while *under* the influence of alcohol.

Under can be used to identify categories:
> **Examples:**
> - You can find her name in the directory *under* the letter P.
> - Porpoises can be found in the encyclopedia *under* mammals.

Until:

Until helps to express the beginning or end of an action, activity, situation or time:
> **Examples:**
> - I'm sorry sir, but the bank is closed. You will not be able to withdraw money *until* tomorrow.
> - (Students taking an exam): Please do not leave your seats *until* the teacher gives you permission.

Up:

Up can mean movement to a higher place:

Examples:
- The price of gasoline has really gone *up*.
- The champagne cork flew *up* into the air when it was removed.

Up can be used to express movement against a current of water:
Examples:
- Salmon always swim *up* stream. (Meaning: against the current of a river or stream)
- We rowed the canoe *up* the river.

Up can be used to express forward movement towards a location further away:
Examples:
- The new park is *up* the road about ten miles and on your right.
- The bikers rode *up* the bike trail another five miles before they stopped and rested.

Up can be used to express forward movement along a route or path:
Examples:
- The truck traveled *up* the road.
- The two friends jogged *up* the path.

Up can be used to express division or cutting of something into pieces:

Examples:
- My mother chopped up the onion and then chopped *up* some garlic and put all the pieces in the sauce.
- The bank robbers divided *up* the money and then ran away.

There are also many other uses for the word *up* in English phrasal verbs and in English expressions (or idioms). Please refer to the Focus on English book about phrasal verbs and the Focus on English book about idioms and expressions (available at your school store or at www.FOEBooks.com.).

Upon:

Upon can be used in many of the same situations where *on* can be used:
Examples:
- *Upon* entering the room, everyone yelled, "surprise!"
- The stone was resting *upon* two supports

With:

With can be used to express things being added on:
Examples:
- I like my tea *with* milk.
- How much is a hamburger *with* French fries.

With is used to express being together or in the company of:
Examples:
- I went *with* my brother to see the show.
- The students went *with* their teacher to the student auditorium.
- Did you see a man *with* a small boy within the last hour?
- Sally came to the party *with* her friend.
- Did you go *with* her?

With is used to express a type of behavior:
Examples:
- They accepted the new jobs *with* gratitude.
- Children have to be handled *with* care.
- The teacher congratulated the class *with* pride.
- The girl was being honest *with* her friend.

With is used to help express feelings:
Examples:
- The office worker was bored *with* her job.
- The newly wed couple were filled *with* joy to be moving into a new home.

With is used to help express affiliation or relationship:
Examples:
- He has been working *with* the International Red Cross for two years.

- Melissa works *with* blind children.

With is used to help express conflict or struggle:
Examples:
- The children are always arguing *with* each other.
- Our football team is going to compete *with* the champion team next week.
- He had trouble *with* the car. The motor wouldn't start.

With is used to help express filling or covering something or an area:
Examples:
- The waitress filled the class *with* water.
- The whole side of the mountain was covered *with* wild flowers.

With helps to express which tool or implement is used to accomplish an action:
Examples:
- The artist painted a picture of the flower *with* his paintbrush.
- The worker dug a hole in the ground *with* a shovel.

With helps to express simultaneous (occurring together at the same time) time and direction:
Examples:
- The teacher always starts the class *with* a quiz.

- The monks always start their day *with* prayer.
- The boat sailed *with* the current.

With helps to express parting or separation:
Examples:
- Toshiko is finished *with* her company and is now looking for a new job.
- She broke up *with* her boyfriend because they didn't spend enough time together.

With helps to express cooperation:
Examples:
- All of the neighbors helped *with* cleaning the park.
- We decided to work *with* them on this important project.
- The car company has decided to form a partnership *with* their main parts manufacturer.
- We no longer do business *with* them.

With helps to express comparisons:
Examples:
- Stefan's shirt didn't go *with* his pants. (Meaning: the colors of his shirt didn't look good *with* the color of his pants.)
- The value of the U.S. dollar is comparable *with* the value of the Canadian dollar. (Meaning: they are approximately equal in value.)

- Two different stores have the computer we want. We should compare one price *with* the other before we buy the computer.

With helps to express reason or cause:
Examples:
- The graduates were smiling *with* joy.
- The man was trembling *with* fear.

There are other uses for the word *with* in English phrasal verbs and in English expressions (or idioms). Please refer to the Focus On English book about phrasal verbs and the Focus on English book about idioms and expressions (available at your school store or from www.FOEBooks.com.).

Within:

Within usually means inside of some area:
Examples:
- *Within* the room there were many fine paintings.
- *Within* the United States there are many fine universities.

Within can be used to express less than a specified period of time:
Examples:
- We should be finished *within* the hour.

- The bus usually comes *within* 15 minutes of the last bus. (Meaning: in less than 15 minutes after the last bus left.)

Within can be used to express less than a specified distance:
Examples:
- The library is *within* two miles of the university.
- We are *within* two miles of our destination.

Without:

Without can mean not having:
Examples:
- She gets to school *without* a car. She walks.
- *Without* your help, I couldn't have finished the project.
- *Without* water, we would not be able to live long.

Without can be used to express the absence of someone or something:
Examples:
- The worker finished the project *without* his colleagues.
- The baby tiger won't survive long *without* its mother.

Without can be used to express the absence of action:
Examples:

- He received a lot of money *without* working.
- She is famous *without* doing anything extraordinary.

Chapter 6 review
*Prepositions beginning with the letters **P** – **T***

*Instructions: read and /or listen carefully to the sentences below. Decide whether the use of the preposition is correct or incorrect. If incorrect, which of these prepositions **best** fits the sentence: **under**, **underneath**, **until**, **up**, **with**, **within**, **without**. The answers can be found in this chapter (above).*

1. Prices of food have really gone up ☐correct ☐incorrect

2. The boats were sailing upon the water. ☐correct ☐incorrect

3. The teacher worked with students to help them understand the new chapter. ☐correct ☐incorrect

4. My friend arrived home with her groceries. I helped my friend until her groceries. ☐correct ☐incorrect

5. Without the help of my family, I could never have finished school. ☐correct ☐incorrect

6. We won't complete the project <u>with</u> next Wednesday.
   ☐correct ☐incorrect

7. Our bus traveled <u>up</u> the highway at high speed.
   ☐correct ☐incorrect

8. The water passes <u>under</u> the bridge. ☐correct ☐incorrect

9. Alice bought the car for <u>under</u> $30,000. ☐correct ☐incorrect

10. Janet finished repairing her car <u>without</u> the help of her brothers. ☐correct ☐incorrect

Appendix

Prepositions following certain common English verbs, by preposition.

About
ask *about*
complain *about*
concerned *about*
crazy *about*
curious *about*
excited *about*
glad *about*
happy *about*
know *about*
nervous *about*
pleased *about*
sad *about*
tell *about*
worried *about*

At
amazed *at*
angry *at*
arrive *at*
awful *at*
good *at*
laugh *at*
mad at
point *at*
slow *at*
surprised *at*
stare *at*
terrible *at*

By
amazed *by*
bored *by*
surprised *by*

For
admire *for*
apologize *for*
apply *for*
ask *for*
bad *for*
excuse *for*
forgive *for*
hope *for*
good *for*
listen *for*
made *for*
look *for*
pay *for*
prepared *for*
qualified *for*
ready *for*
responsible *for*
search *for*
feel sorry *for*
thank *for*
wait *for*

From
absent *from*
borrow *from*
different *from*
divorced *from*
escape *from*
exhausted *from*
gone *from*
hear *from*
hide *from*

Page 174

safe *from*
separate *from*
tired *from*

In
arrive *in*
believe *in*
interested *in*

Into
divide *into*

Of
afraid *of*
ashamed *of*
approve *of*
aware *of*
careful *of*
composed *of*
consist *of*
dream *of*
fond *of*
frightened *of*
full *of*
get rid *of*
proud *of*
scared *of*
sick *of*
sure *of*
take care *of*
terrified *of*
tired *of*

To
accustomed *to*
apply *to*
belong *to*
compare *to*
complain *to*
devoted *to*
engaged *to*
equal *to*
happen *to*
introduce *to*
invite *to*
kind *to*
listen *to*
married *to*
matter *to*
add *to*
nice *to*
opposed *to*
polite *to*
related *to*
similar *to*
speak *to*
travel *to*

With
acquainted *with*
agree *with*
angry *with*
argue *with*
compare *with*
disagree *with*
discuss *with*
familiar *with*
friendly *with*
help *with*
patient *with*
pleased *with*
satisfied *with*
talk *with*

INDEX

- about, 90
- above, 12, 91
- absent *from*, 39
- accustomed *to*, 39
- acquainted *with*, 40
- across, 12, 93
- add (this) *to* (that), 68
- admire *for*, 40
- afraid *of*, 40
- after, 12, 93
- against, 13, 95
- agree *with*, 40
- ahead of, 96
- along, 14, 23, 96
- amazed *at* / *by*, 41
- among, 14, 97
- angry *at* / *with*, 41
- apologize *for* / *to*, 41

- apply *to* / *for*, 42
- approve *of*, 42
- argue *with*, 42
- around, 14, 28, 97
- arrive *at* or *in*, 42
- as, 98
- ashamed *of*, 41
- ask *for* or *about*, 43
- at, 2, 15, 28, 98
- aware *of*, 43
- awful *at*, 43
- bad *for*, 45
- before, 100
- behind, 15, 101
- believe *in*, 45
- belong *to*, 45
- below, 16, 101
- beneath, 16, 102
- beside, 13, 102

Page 177

Index

- besides, 102
- between, 23, 103
- beyond, 105
- bored with / by, 45
- borrow *from*, 46
- by, 7, 22, 31, 32, 106
- careful *of*, 46
- close to, 110
- compare *to* / *with*, 46
- complain *to* / *about*, 46
- composed *of*, 47
- concentrate *on*, 47
- concerned *about*, 47
- consist *of*, 47
- content *with*, 48
- crazy *about*, 48
- curious *about*, 48
- depend *on*, 51
- despite, 111
- devoted *to*, 51
- different *from*, 51
- disagree *with*, 52
- disappointed *in*, 52
- discuss *with*, 52
- divide (this) *by* (that), 69
- divide *into*, 52
- divorced *from*, 52
- down, 111
- dream *of*, 53
- during, 6, 112
- engaged *to*, 53
- equal *to*, 53
- escape *from*, 53
- excited *about*, 54
- excuse *for*, 54
- exhausted *from*, 54
- familiar *with*, 54
- far from, 112
- fond *of*, 57
- for, 7, 113
- forgive *for*, 57

Index

- friendly *with* / *to*, 57
- frightened *of* / *by*, 58
- from, 7, 23, 115
- full *of*, 58
- get rid *of*, 58
- glad *about*, 58
- gone *from*, 59
- good *at*, 58
- good *for*, 59
- graduate *from*, 59
- happen *to*, 59
- hear *about*, 60
- hear *from*, 60
- help *with*, 60
- hide *from*, 60
- hope *for*, 61
- in back of, 123
- in front of, 124
- in, 3, 15, 21, 26, 120
- inside, 22, 124
- insist *on*, 61

- instead of, 124
- interested *in*, 61
- into, 21, 125
- introduce *to*, 62
- invite *to*, 62
- involved *in* / *with*, 62
- kind *to*, 65
- know *about*, 65
- laugh *at*, 65
- like, 126
- listen *to* / *for*, 66
- look *at* / *for*, 66
- look forward *to*, 66
- mad *at*, 67
- made *for*, 67
- made *of*, 67
- married *to*, 67
- matter *to*, 67
- multiply (this) *by* (that), 68
- near, 27, 127

Page 179

Index

- nervous *about*, 71
- next to, 127
- nice *to*, 71
- of, 130
- off, 22, 132
- on, 2, 16, 21, 27, 134
- onto, 139
- opposed *to*, 71
- opposite, 139
- out, 140
- outside, 143
- over, 6, 143
- past, 148
- patient *with*, 72
- pay *for*, 72
- pleased *with* / *about*, 72
- point *at*, 72
- polite *to*, 72
- prepared *for*, 73

- protect (something / someone) *from*, 73
- proud *of*, 73
- qualified *for*, 73
- ready *for*, 76
- related *to*, 76
- rely *on*, 76
- responsible *for*, 77
- sad *about*, 77
- safe *from*, 77
- satisfied *with*, 78
- scared *of* / *by*, 78
- search *for*, 78
- separate *from*, 78
- sick *of*, 79
- similar *to*, 79
- since, 7, 149
- slow *at*, 79
- sorry *for*, 80
- speak *to* (someone) *about*, 80

Index

- stare *at*, 80
- subtract (this) *from* (that), 68
- sure *of*, 81
- surprise d *at* / *by*, 79
- take care *of*, 83
- talk *to* / *with*, 83
- tell *about*, 83
- terrible *at*, 84
- terrified *by* / *of*, 84
- thank *for*, 84
- through, 149
- throughout, 152
- tired *from*, 84
- tired *of*, 84

- to, 127
- to, 152
- toward(s), 26, 157
- travel *to*, 85
- under, 6, 16, 161
- underneath, 162
- until, 163
- up, 163
- upon, 165
- used *to*, 85
- wait *for*, 85
- wait *on*, 85
- with, 31, 34, 165
- within, 5, 169
- without. 170
- worried *about*, 86

Page 181

Other Focus on English books available:

- *Beyond Phrasal Verbs: Mastering Phrasal Verbs in Context*
- *Idioms and Expressions for Real English Communication*
- *Mastering Gerunds and Infinitives for ESL Learners.*
- *Learn and Remember Irregular English Verbs*
- *English Articles A, AN, and THE: Use Them Correctly in Every English Sentence.*
- *Mastering 6 English Hotspots for ESL Learners*

NOTES

NOTES